on track ...

Saga

every album, every song

Mike Wilson

SONICBOND

sonicbondpublishing.com

Sonicbond Publishing Limited
www.sonicbondpublishing.co.uk
Email: info@sonicbondpublishing.co.uk

First Published in the United Kingdom 2026
First Published in the United States 2026

British Library Cataloguing in Publication Data:
A Catalogue record for this book is available from the British Library

ISBN 978-1-78952-376-8

Typeset in ITC Garamond Std & ITC Avant Garde Gothic
Printed and bound in England

Graphic design and typesetting: Full Moon Media

Cover photograph of Ian Crichton by Stêphan Hill

Follow us on social media:
Twitter: https://twitter.com/SonicbondP
Instagram: www.instagram.com/sonicbondpublishing_/
Facebook: www.facebook.com/SonicbondPublishing/

Linktree QR code:

'From Saga to Symmetry'

For Ross, Rob, Baz and Kevin

Thanks To

My wife Alison for sharing my musical adventures, including when we first saw the mighty Saga on 10 November 1983 and for supporting all my many projects, this book being yet another one. To my son, Adam and daughter Hannah and to Kim, Jennifer, Abigail and Andy.

For making life much easier in the creation of this book.

Mark Marrington, Russ Hepworth-Sawyer, Martin Popoff, Bob Wegner and, from Sonicbond Publishing, Stephen Lambe and Dominic Sanderson, for having faith and patience. Your support has been invaluable.

on track ...
Saga

Contents

Authors Notes

The contents within this book have been taken from a variety of sources, including my own personal collection of *Kerrang!* and the more recent *Prog* and *Classic Rock*. Matthias Mineur's liner notes on the 2021 reissues have also provided useful insights, but the most significant and essential resource is the book *Saga The Biography* by Edwin Ammerlaan, published in 2008. I'm extremely grateful to Edwin for his kind support in supplying additional material and photographs and for introducing me to Bert Treep, who has also graciously shared his ideas and photographs. Thanks to Peter Joe Hulmes for lending me the stuff I didn't already have.

Penny Crichton has also been incredibly generous in supplying some of her own fantastic images, including the front cover album designs. Thanks to Ian Crichton for the cover photograph, to Nicole Negus for your help and Steve Negus and Jim Crichton for their time and honesty during our chats. It was an honour to meet you both.

All quotes, unless otherwise noted, are taken from the book *Saga The Biography* by Edwin Ammerlaan. Matthias Mineur's quotes are taken from the sleeve notes of the 2021 reissues.

Saga And Me

It's 1980 and I'm the 20-year-old drummer in the heavy rock band Oxym. We were always trying to outdo each other by discovering new and better acts. Phil (Lord) had already introduced us to UFO, Scorpions and Judas Priest, Rob (Rigby) to Horslips and Lindisfarne – so an eclectic mix. Being born and bred in Accrington, I was aware of the heritage of one of prog's finest, but didn't really appreciate Jon Anderson and Yes until a bit later.

Whilst searching in a local record shop, I came across an interesting album cover from a band I'd never heard of. The cover had incredible artwork, a prehistoric creature that had just snapped the top off a building and was flying out to sea. There were no photographs of the band, but I was intrigued enough and at £2.99 for a tatty copy, I had a punt. *Images At Twilight* and Saga were mine.

The first track I heard was therefore 'It's Time (Chapter Three)'. Four minutes and one second that I'll never forget. This was only Saga's second album and I soon found their first and continued to collect everything they did from then on. Unusually, I hadn't seen any mention of Saga in the music press, not even from Geoff Barton in *Sounds*. My then-album collection mainly consisted of his recommendations, so this truly was a spectacular find. Saga became the band that I grew up with and I eagerly awaited each release. They didn't tour that much in the UK, but I was fortunate to see them three times, all in London, one of these being on the *Full Circle* tour when, thanks to a roadie, I managed to get backstage to have my poster signed. The first and only time I met Saga.

In 2022, my daughter, Hannah, secretly wrote to all the bands that she knew I was a fan of, asking if they'd be kind enough to wish Alison and me all the best for our 40th wedding anniversary. Saga were included and their response was, 'Hello, Hannah. Thank you for contacting us. Your message has been sent to the band and you should receive a reply at some point soon.' She didn't. The three people who did send congratulatory videos were Neil Carter (UFO, Wild Horses), John Mitchell (Lonely Robot, Arena, It Bites) and Ian Anderson (Jethro Tull).

Despite this minor 'setback', it's a privilege to compile this book and to further research and analyse Saga's journey and their songs, noting how they successfully evolved over the last 49 years.

It's Time

As I write, Saga have just completed their *It Never Ends* tour, playing 40 dates from 3 February 2024 to 7 December 2024, which is remarkable for a band in their 47th year. From the 'classic' lineup, Steve Negus (drums) left Saga in 2003 to pursue his own musical endeavours, Jim Crichton (bass) retired from touring in 2018 and Ian Crichton (guitar) took time off due to a broken leg. Jim Gilmour (keyboards) was still going strong and as enthusiastically as ever and there is nothing but respect to Michael Sadler (vocals) for his bravery, dedication and sheer willingness not to let down his fans. Sadler was diagnosed with a rare form of cancer and had an operation mid-tour. Only two shows were cancelled. The man is amazing.

As detailed in Edwin Ammerlaan's incredible *Saga The Biography,* in their first 30 years, Saga sold over eight million albums, were the first rock band to release a fully digital live CD, were the first Canadian act to perform behind the Iron Curtain and played in more than 20 countries to over 15 million people. The next 18 years were more challenging, but they continued to sell out venues in Germany and Europe, even though the albums gradually dried up. Their significant back catalogue could, it would seem, sustain them forever in these territories.

So, who are Saga? Lorriane Le Page from the *St Catherine's Standard*, writing on 28 October 1981, summed them up beautifully:

> Saga's music is undeniably rooted in rock with a mixture of blues and funk injected into their rhythmic veins. A good use of keyboards provides a majestic sound that has both bite and clarity. The overall sound is lush, yet hard and intense; it assaults, while at the same time woos the ear as well as the soul.

Michael Sadler spoke to Alex Varty of *Vancouver Free Press* in 1980:

> We will take very melodic passages, which, if they were played in a light way, could be considered very classical or ethereal and put interesting rhythms and bottom ends underneath them. That's really the sum total of what our music is about, combining the important 'body music' element with tasteful full chordal passages. And then we'll add lots of hot guitar lines on top.

Laura Canyon said this to *Kerrang!* on 10 February 1983:

> They've got class, not to mention melody, grandness, pomp, texture, sophistication, skill, versatility, baroque and enough keyboards and synthesisers to open up a shop and still have enough to start a futurist band. Stick Rush, Pink Floyd and Phil Spector in a recording studio, don't let them take too many drugs and it will come out sounding like Saga.

Saga's first lineup formed in 1977 and consisted of bass player Jim Crichton, his brother Ian on guitar, vocalist Michael Sadler, drummer Steve Negus and keyboard player Peter Rochon. The Crichtons, originally from Scotland, moved to Oakville, Ontario. Michael Sadler moved to Canada from Wales when he was three years old. Steve Negus is from Hamilton, less than 20 miles away from Oakville and Peter Rochon is from the same area.

Sadler, who had sung in a choir in his younger days, left school at 16 and joined a blues band, Talas (originally Terraplane), becoming their vocalist and bass player. The band's drummer had a copy of *Three Friends* by Gentle Giant, which made a massive impression on Sadler and he vowed to 'make music like that'.

Jim Crichton listened to classical music but also to prog bands such as Genesis and decided to learn the guitar. He bought his first one at the age of 13 and eventually joined a band that already had a guitarist. Their teenage manager threatened that if he didn't play bass, he'd be fired. So he did.

Ian Crichton was drawn to music through his older brother and at the age of 12 would borrow his bass guitar. Jim persuaded him to buy a cheap guitar so that he could have his bass back. Ian did and began to listen to Jeff Beck, Jimmy Page and Jimi Hendrix, learning their techniques. He saved up to buy a white Fender Stratocaster, the instrument he used on the first three Saga albums. After playing the Toronto circuit with random gigs and in supportive roles, he joined his first band, Kickback, whose set included Led Zeppelin and Trapeze covers.

Jim answered an advert he saw in a local newspaper for the band Truck, formerly Heat Exchange, who had recorded an album that wasn't released; they were thought to be too progressive. They reformed as Truck, having been renamed by Peter Francey, the manager of a previous version of Truck, who had the rights to the name and their equipment and a bus. Truck played progressive rock, a mix of originals and covers, including King Crimson and Gentle Giant. Truck was the first band that Jim Crichton started to make a living with.

Whilst preparing for a gig in Hamilton in 1971, Sadler's Talas borrowed a Mellotron from Truck as theirs had broken down, an arrangement that instigated Sadler and Crichton's first meeting. Sadler became Truck's singer when the original vocalist left. Truck concentrated on live performances, therefore no vinyl releases and they split up due to financial difficulties. A disillusioned Sadler got out of the music business for the next 18 months.

Meanwhile, Jim got a call from another band, Fludd, who offered him more opportunities and money. In that band were Steve Negus and Peter Rochon. The band had previously made five albums and 14 singles. Jim is on some of the singles, but joined just after they'd made their last album. The band's roots went back to the mid-1960s.

Steve Negus was ten years old when he wanted to play drums and got his first kit at 12. Six years later, he joined rock 'n' roll band Bananas before forming his own band, Shelter and then joining Fullerton Dam, who were signed to Condor Records and had released one album, *Breaks*, in 1976. Fludd, who were after a drummer, went to see Fullerton Dam in concert, seeking out Negus and he accepted the offer to join them.

Jim Crichton ended his journey touring with Fludd and began experimenting with some new songs using a Mini-Moog as one of the main instruments. At the time, there were no polyphonic synthesisers available, so he had to play each note one at a time to create the musical parts. After completing a number of rough arrangements, he called Sadler and convinced him to come over to sing on a few of the songs. Sadler came to Crichton's home and never left. They continued to write together, creating the ingredients that would form Saga's first album.

They wrote 20 songs together on a four-track recorder and used cardboard boxes for drums and were soon ready to form a band, so they called upon Negus, Rochon and Ian Crichton, who left Kickback to join them. Originally called Pockets, the quintet amassed 23 songs in six months and performed their first gig, a set of original songs, on 13 June 1977 at the Tudor Tavern, Cambridge, Ontario, to about 40 people. They continued to play more gigs on the Toronto club circuit and were ready to record their first album. Through Peter Rochon, they were introduced to Phase One producer Paul Gross. Gross and Rochon had been in a band called Wishbone. Fludd had also used Phase One Studio in Scarborough, Ontario. Gross helped to finance the first album and produced the band's first three releases.

With the debut album in the making, they became aware of an American band also called Pockets. Jim Crichton was working on the Chapters concept, a song-based story/puzzle, so with this in mind, they renamed themselves Saga.

Big In Germany

Saga have fans all over the world, but were particularly popular in Puerto Rico and Europe. Their spiritual home, however, is Germany, where the vast majority of their live releases were recorded. Jim Crichton told Howard Johnson of *Kerrang!* in October 1983:

> It all started when a chain of record stores in Canada exported 50 copies of our first album to Germany. They sold immediately, so more went out. We shifted 10,000 copies without a label deal, which was amazing. The response was so strong that a chain of stores in Germany had their own posters printed, which led to our deal with Deutsche Grammophon. In our first year, we had success in Canada, Germany and Puerto Rico, but we couldn't figure out why.

Chapters

Sixteen of Saga's songs have been designated 'Chapters', a puzzle devised by Jim Crichton. Eight are spread across the first four albums and the other eight appear again from 1999. Crichton explains:

> This has become an important thread across the Saga albums and continues to intrigue fans across the world, who are still trying to figure it out. No other band had done anything like this. The 'Chapters' contain many lyrical secrets, the aim being that they could be deciphered as a complete story.

The band were keen to emphasise that this was not a gimmick. It's a very clever and forward-thinking concept, which I suspect kept fans engaged and intrigued right up until the final one, 'Worlds Apart (Chapter 16)', on *Marathon*.

In 1981, Crichton explained to Max Blake of *UK Trax* that the concept is set in a futuristic time. Earth is undergoing destruction and is rescued from total collapse by an alien race, whose physical features are depicted on the album covers. The dragonfly alien creature evolved and morphed over the years and was affectionately known as 'Golden Boy', aka Harold.

In 2005, Saga released *Chapters Live*, a CD containing each of the 16 'Chapters' in number order. This finally revealed the whole story and its references to politics, culture and religion. Jim Crichton:

> The process was created in 1978 for eight 'Chapter' songs to be released purposely mixed up to create a puzzle and to ensure that at least the band got a four-album deal. It could be the only 'album' that took over 28 years to write and record.

Two main ingredients inspired the story: the Cold War and an article Crichton read about how Albert Einstein's brain had been preserved and was residing at the home of the pathologist Thomas S. Harvey, MD, who performed the autopsy in 1955. 'The idea that it may be possible to still tap into the mind of the man who unlocked the mystery of the atom, with his brain on the shelf in someone's house, sparked the idea for the 'Chapters'. Jim Crichton, 'This helped to pull the Saga albums together and when we stopped doing them, it lost some of the atmosphere.'

Reissues

Worthy of mention are SPV's 2002/2003 CD reissues, superbly remastered by Steve Negus with new features and bonus tracks. In 2021, celebrating 40 years of Saga, earMusic reissued the first 17 studio albums and the first two live albums on CD and vinyl, mastered by Eike Freese. They include additional liner notes from individual band members and an excellent overview of each album by Matthias Mineur. Many of these are captured on vinyl for the first time, but all are extremely impressive, very collectable and worth the cost of replenishing your stock or starting your Saga collection.

Saga (1978)

Personnel:
Michael Sadler: lead vocal, keyboard, Moogs
Jim Crichton: bass, Moog bass
Peter Rochon: lead keyboards, vocals, Moogs
Ian Crichton: all guitars
Steve Negus: drums, percussion, Moog drum
Arranged by Saga
Recorded at Phase One Studios, Toronto, Canada
Produced by Paul Gross
Engineered and mixed by Alan Thorne (mixing engineer on 'Ice Nice': Mark Wright)
Album concept and design by Zoran Busic
Illustration by Rene Zamic
Release date: 8 April 1978
Label: Maze Records
Running time: 46:04
Highest chart places: Sweden: 33, UK: did not chart, US: did not chart, CN: did not chart

Saga had toured the Toronto club circuit extensively, amassing an impressive number of songs, eight of which were selected for the first album. Phase One studio, built by producer Paul Gross in 1974, was chosen. Gross, who helped the band financially and musically, had 'fallen in love' with their music.

Gross has fond memories of recording *Saga* using all the available equipment and facilities with engineer Alan Thorne, an Australian who'd been working at Trident studios in England on sessions with *Queen* and *John Lennon*. In 1978, there were no plug-ins, so effects were created manually and required a high level of creativity. Gross, influenced by Alan Parsons, Queen and Supertramp, was keen to give Saga their own sound by making the instruments more orchestrated using reverb and other available effects. He encouraged the band to perform as they wished and to the best of their individual abilities, recalling that the recording was an adventure and it was exciting to break every recording rule, such as recording vocals in the back seat of a car and mic'ing up a barbecue for sound effects. Jim Crichton remembers that the songwriting process involved recording one note at a time on a Micromoog because polyphonic synthesisers weren't available. Fortunately, the Polymoog came just in time for the recording session and subsequent tours.

The band chose to offer PolyGram Canada the demos as the finished master and all they had to do was press and sell the vinyl. Unfortunately, they were also promoting the soundtrack to *Saturday Night Fever*, which became one of the best-selling pop music albums ever. Needless to say, Saga didn't get the attention they needed.

The album was also initially hampered by the weakness of the Canadian dollar and a lack of interest amongst North American labels. European importers saw this differently and one from Germany shipped 10,000 copies without a deal, sparking widespread interest across Europe. Polydor Europe pressed more vinyl locally and sold over 35,000 copies, a staggering amount considering that Saga's prog-oriented style was hard to categorise, not to mention the lack of real promotion or airplay.

Saga were up against a feast of classic albums in 1978, including *UK* by UK, *And Then There Were Three* by Genesis, *Hemispheres* by Rush, *Heavy Horses* by Jethro Tull and *Tormato* by Yes. But as a debut album, this is a mighty fine piece of work and sets the musical template for the next two releases, which showcase similar styles, dominated by solid keyboard riffs and melodies and bright, powerful production values delivered by Gross.

'How Long?' (4.01) (J. Crichton, Sadler, Rochon)
The first thing that strikes you is the power and clarity. Negus recalls that he was one of the first people to use a Moog drum, which he continued to use until he favoured the Simmons kit on *Worlds Apart*. The opener is an instantly appealing number, combining rock energy with catchy pop melodies and a heavy emphasis on synthesisers, but it's the guitar riff that hits you between the ears, being a simple but instantly memorable motif. This and sequenced keyboards open for the first bars and repeat throughout. 'You thought you had it in the bag, thought you had it all figured out', belts out Michael Sadler, also the lyricist, implying a lack of acceptance of a current situation and a reluctance to move on. The chorus consists of punctuated phrasing, sublime drum fills and Sadler asking, 'How long did your dream carry on, how long did your dream spin around'. At 3.03, we're back to the main riff and then a dead stop to end. There are no solos, but it's an impressively heavy start and an immense track to launch your career. It featured on three singles, with respective B-sides being 'Climbing The Ladder', 'Humble Stance' and 'On The Loose'.

'Humble Stance' (5.46) (J. Crichton, Sadler, Rochon, I. Crichton)
This track appears on almost all the band's live albums and DVDs and was probably played at every live performance they've ever done. When performing live, Sadler plays bass and Jim Crichton is on keyboards. It is indeed a classic amongst Saga fans, with lyrics by Jim Crichton, sung with conviction by Sadler. 'Lately I've been watching a little complex grow' starts the first verse, ending with 'There's no one going to help you'. It's an observational and advisory tale looking at the subject from a third-party perspective. Musically, it's another powerful statement, the strength being the drum pattern, a 'cut-time shuffle' according to Negus and clever fills executed with precision based on Negus's R&B roots. Crichton's bass locks in superbly.

Rochon begins the track with an evocative keyboard intro followed by his signature hum-along melody, complementing the 'double-tracked' vocal from Sadler. A change of tempo at 1.45 sees Sadler demonstrating his more choral versatility, but it's not until 3.06 that the song really takes off with a full-on instrumental assault, giving the opportunity for Rochon, then Ian Crichton, to solo individually, then in unison. For a first album in particular, this is mightily impressive stuff and well worth witnessing live and is a fitting tribute to Rochon on his only Saga album. Negus described him as more of a funk player, like himself, as perfectly demonstrated in this superb song.

'Climbing The Ladder' (4.44) (J. Crichton, Sadler, Rochon, I. Crichton)
'Humble Stance' provides the perfect ending, a fade out and a slight gap before Crichton's tastefully textured guitar introduces track three, an upbeat and energetic number. The lyrics are again by Sadler, with a more evident chorus this time: 'Climbing the ladder, three rungs forward, two rungs back, climbing the ladder, trying to stay on just the right track' – a descriptive story about dreams and ambitions. Guitars and keyboards ebb and flow over a solid rhythm courtesy of Negus and Crichton. The next instrumental passage at 1.52 is dominated by Rochon's synthesiser before another change at 3.19, with guitar and keyboards weaving the melody tightly together over a four on the floor bass drum. Rochon's keyboard is then left alone to steer the track to its finish. Despite being another very good song that cleverly builds momentum, it's not favoured by the band, it would seem, as it doesn't feature on any live release. A pity.

'Will It Be You? (Chapter Four)' (7.11) (J. Crichton, Sadler, Rochon, Crichton, Negus)
Closing side one is the first of the initial eight 'Chapter' songs and the longest track on the album. It explores futuristic themes of destiny and identity, posing the question of who will be chosen: 'All the ships have arrived, we know that only one will survive, will it be me, will it be you'. It's a strong song and an ideal demonstration of Saga's expertise in stripping a song down to its basics and building it back up again, adding one instrument at a time. Noticeable is Crichton's tight, chugging guitar during the instrumental sections. It's not Saga's most famous or popular song, but it's well constructed, with sharp, urgent keyboard figures that reinforce the title's lyrical questioning and mirror the story's atmospheric theme of doubt and anticipation. It also appears on *Chapters Live* and *So Good So Far*, where the harmonies are astonishing.

'The Perfectionist' (5.43) (J. Crichton, Sadler)
A crowd favourite with lyrics by Jim Crichton and featuring one Ellery Sneed, a chap whose pursuit of perfection ultimately isolates him from others. He develops a plan and decides that 'not a friend could remain to witness his

death, so a terminal wine he would treat', 'The plan was to hold a very large feast, serving the wine at the end'. So, he will ensure that no one will be left behind to remember his self-proclaimed imperfections or witness his final moments and it's macabre and disturbing stuff, which would do well as a *Tales Of The Unexpected* plot. A pleasant keyboard introduction by Rochon signals the rest of the band to join him. It's controlled and laid back as Sadler begins the tale and ominously sings some terrifically sharp lines. Rochon plays the track's melody beautifully and the piano solo segment is particularly effective, capturing the eerie essence of the song and leading to the subsequent build-up of heart-beating drums and increasing volume to get back to the next verse. Overall, the complex keyboard arrangement, driving beat and frequent stabs mirror the tension and intensity associated with striving for perfection. Much admired also by the band, they reintroduced it acoustically on *Symmetry* 43 years later.

'Give 'Em The Money' (4.24) (J. Crichton, Sadler)
A satirical take on the pursuit of wealth, materialism, greed and the satisfaction it brings. Saga successfully combine a direct, riff-driven rock foundation with understated touches of layered keyboards. It begins with a quiet, almost menacing intro and Sadler practically whispering Jim Crichton's lyrics. Instrumentally, it begins softly, then picks up a notch at the chorus, which repeats 'Give 'em the money less work more pay'. At 2.16, there's an aggressive twist as the subtleties of the opening refrain are replaced by a punchy riff from Ian Crichton, which builds to the chorus before another change of dynamic, featuring a prominent bassline laying the foundation for Rochon's impressive soloing, transitioning superbly through both speakers. This is not the strongest song on the album, but there's enough going on to make it interesting and it sits well amongst its peers. It only appears live on *Worlds Apart Revisited*, but it does deserve better.

'Ice Nice' (6.53) (J. Crichton)
The only song on the album solely written by Jim Crichton that explores themes of coldness and emotional distance. Crichton is sticking to the money theme: 'Ice, Nice, everything's twice as bright with money in your hands'. Musically, it has a similar feel to the opening of the previous track, played and sung in almost the same way. It's got an atmospheric, reflective and haunting melody, with 'Ice, Nice' whispered. 'How long have you been listening' could perhaps be a nod to track one. Saga had a knack for cleverly referencing their song titles in some of their other tracks and continued to do this throughout their career. At four minutes, the band's tendency to change tempos and build dynamics manifests itself. The back beat just on the count of four adds tension and then at 5.38, all hell is nearly let loose, with some clever interplay between guitar and keyboards and a solid syncopated bass. The number also came to life when performed live, with Sadler playing the piano intro.

'Tired World (Chapter Six)' (7.05) (J. Crichton, Sadler, Rochon, I. Crichton, Negus)
It's another 'Chapters' track and Jim Crichton explains that the pollution on Earth is getting worse every year and the world is tiring. The lyrics therefore reflect a world weary from conflict and struggle, 'A vision of buildings sitting empty, there's not a person to be found'. Musically, it also evokes a sense of both despair and hope, led by a piano intro and an effective use of synthesiser throughout. The rhythm has a half-time feel during the verse and there are some tasteful drum fills, Negus also using his toms and open hi hat efficiently. The chorus is more staccato, emphasising the phrasing 'A sleeping world, just waiting, a tired world'. During the lengthy middle-eight to the end, Ian Crichton, too low in the mix, delivers an impressive solo, a taster of his capabilities to be showcased more in the future, with a combination of phrasing and intricate fretwork. An ideal track to end a solid debut album, setting a marker for the future. It also features acoustically on *Symmetry* and is frequently performed live, where Crichton is in shredding heaven.

Images At Twilight (1979)

Personnel:
Michael Sadler: lead vocal, keyboard, Moogs
Jim Crichton: bass guitar, Moog bass
Greg Chadd: keyboards, vocals, vocoder, Moogs
Ian Crichton: acoustic and electric guitars
Steve Negus: drums, percussion
Arranged by Saga
Recorded at Phase One Studios, Toronto, Canada
Produced by Paul Gross
Recording engineers: Alan Thorne and Mick Walsh
Album concept and design: Zoran Busic
Illustration by Tony Roberts, Young Artists, London, England
Photos by Terry Hrynyk and Rosemary Miller
Running time: 36.37
Release date: October 1979
Label: Maze Records and Polydor
Highest chart places: did not chart in any territory

Following the unexpected success of *Saga,* it was time for more songs to be committed to vinyl using the same formula of Paul Gross, his studio and Alan Thorne. Sadler observed that they weren't under the normal pressure to record the album, 'unlike Boston, who had a multi-million-selling first album.'

Months before the recording session was to commence, with most of the demos completed, Rochon announced he was to leave. He needed a steady income, which couldn't be guaranteed playing in a band. Saga were sad to see him go and the parting was friendly. Steve Negus told me that Rochon was highly regarded by the band, as a musician and human and that he'd kept in touch with him.

Following a recommendation from Max Webster's drummer, Gary McCracken (who I've had a drum lesson from), Greg Chadd joined Saga in December 1978 and gigged and recorded until August 1979 before he left for personal, professional and business reasons.

The album is a natural progression from the debut, being rockier but still heavily weighted towards keyboard riffing, this time allowing Ian Crichton the space to showcase his exceptional guitar skills. He said, 'I had a hard time getting my guitar in; we discussed how much guitar should be used. I was 22 years old and started to get used to being in a studio, getting better guitar tones, mics on amps, etc.'

Taken from the liner notes of *Synopsis*, a special low-price EP, Malcolm Dome from *Record Mirror* on 21 June 1980 wrote:

> You know how it is, an album arrives unexpectedly through the post from a band with whom you are not familiar, so onto the jolly old turntable it goes

and suddenly WHAMMO! You realise what you've got is an absolute classic. *Images At Twilight*, their first UK release, is, for all that, a masterpiece. Each and every note is perfectly thought out and executed, yet none of the eight compositions happily ever drift into the zone of bland plateau. Rock with all the peaks and troughs of emotion eradicated from the mix.

Sadler: 'Even the biggest radio stations in our home country thought we were a German band because we'd had our first big hits in Europe, whereas back home we were still an insider tip. The album is not perfect, but is any record ever? We don't make any compromises, we just tried loads of different stuff' (taken from *Noisecreep.com*).

In June 1980, Saga set off for their first European tour supporting Styx and they were also nominated for a Juno Award. The album proved to be the perfect sequel to their debut, harder and more compact. The SPV CD 2002 reissue bonus is 'It's Time (Live Video Track)'.

'It's Time (Chapter Three)' (4.07) (J. Crichton, Sadler, I. Crichton, Negus, Chadd)

Side one opens with a full band composition, including contributions from new keyboard player Greg Chadd, with lyrics by Jim Crichton. It is the best track on the album and it's a 'Chapter'. The track opens with four bars of the track's signature theme on keyboard as Negus keeps a steady four on the floor beneath Jim Crichton's basslines. Next up is a tight and tasteful stab sequence that introduces the vocal: 'Large and tall ones, short and small ones working round a frame', Sadler's distinctive tones ring out crystal clear and are sung with purpose. Throughout the verse, Chadd plays a staccato motif and the track powers along as Ian Crichton solos expertly with good use of controlled feedback. At 1.20, we're into the bombastic chorus: 'It's Time, this time, make me now, it's time this time, change me now'. The second verse has a clever keyboard pattern in the background and at the end of each line, a bouncing bass is a perfect accompaniment to the solid rock feel of the song. This radio-friendly track was released as a single, reaching number 12 in the Canadian charts, with the B-sides 'Mouse In A Maze' and 'See Them Smile'.

'See Them Smile' (3.28) (J. Crichton)

One of the more accessible tracks with a strong presence from both synthesiser and guitar. Chadd leads in with a quirky, singular staccato piano prior to the band playing an instrumental version of the chorus melody, another recognisable Saga trait. There's a constant keyboard pattern keeping the pace, the guitar line being less fluid, focusing on accenting with the exceptionally tight bass and drums. The multilayered chorus is memorable, simple, but catchy and Chadd tries out a vocoder, a device that creates a synthesised vocal effect. The verses consist of a series of stabbed phrases over which Sadler references 'winter tan's, 'Gucci shoes', 'Jaguar rentals', 'bank accounts', a 'TV' and a 'credit card'. No prog fantasy tales here – just financial management and a third party observing someone wasting their cash: 'They'll watch you spend your money, see them smile'. It's a clever and thought-provoking reference to material wealth. This terrific number rarely appeared live but did surface as a single with 'Mouse In A Maze' as the B-side.

'Slow Motion' (3.56) (Sadler, J. Crichton)
The track starts with an arpeggio sequencer panning across left and right before the chorus melody comes in with an open hi hat pattern. The verses have a completely different feel than the previous two tracks, a rhythm described by Sadler as a 'rock waltz', the beat coming in at halftime. There isn't a dramatic change going into the chorus, but the groove is in 4/4 time and the pace seems to pick up slightly. The bassline follows the vocal melody, with Sadler singing at his most soulful so far. The beat and fills have an appealing calypso feel, making the track more unusual than previous offerings. Effects are added to the vocals, like an old wireless, before the track fades out to a satisfying conclusion. It's the only track from *Images* that doesn't appear on any live recording, but it was released as a single with 'Careful Where You Step' as the B-side. Ian Crichton told Michael Walmsley of *The Ontarian* newspaper in January 1980 that the track 'is the most hit-oriented on the album.'

'You're Not Alone' (5.28) (J. Crichton, I. Crichton, Negus, Rochon)
The last track on side one is an absolute classic, one of Saga's finest, featuring on virtually all their live releases and on several of the 'greatest hits' albums. The carefully observed lyrics suggest that there's no need to face things alone. Interestingly, this was written by all the band except Sadler, but he's the one who expertly uses the arrangement to great effect for audience participation time when in concert, running from one side of the stage to the other to get responses, 'You're not, you're not, you're not alone'.

The track was conceived during Peter Rochon's tenure and so he's credited for his contribution. It kicks off unusually with a lone guitar riff followed by a tricky off-beat drum combination creating an odd time illusion. A short single stroke roll burst heralds the first verse and again, we're introduced to a completely different rhythm. The track is in 4/4, but the backbeat is not standard 2 and 4, giving it a strange but appealing feel, classic Negus. Alternating vocals between Sadler and Chadd lead into the sing-along chorus and a dead stop at 2.21 allows the song to reset before it fluctuates instrumentally through multiple layers, at one point leaving just a sustained keyboard and a 16th note hi-hat pattern. Live, this is the audience participation bit. At 3.09, it's the same middle eight but with a funked-up ride pattern and full throttle keyboards for a lengthy orchestral-themed break before another round of stabs. This section continues to build until Crichton enters the fray with the most dynamic of guitar solos. A revamped version appears on *The Pleasure And The Pain*. It's so popular live that Sadler would just ask the audience, 'You know what to do, right?'

'Take It Or Leave It' (4.03) (Sadler, J. Crichton)
Saga return to a more upbeat, rock-oriented track with a catchy, straightforward structure and sharp, punchy riffs. There's a nice balance between the straightforward rock elements and the more intricate keyboard lines. The song could well be about putting the words together for this track: 'Once again he lays his head down and rubs his tired eyes' ... 'There are so many different ways to say exactly what he means within a simple phrase'. There are four bars of the introductory section, with all the band playing, before a brief stop featuring staccato keyboards, then it's into the first verse, with Sadler's tone and phrasing more mournful and added harmonies at the end of each line. The chorus is upbeat and very chantable: 'Take it or leave it, you're going to have to read between the lines'. Following another verse and chorus, the middle eight starts with a pause and Crichton expertly solos under the track's main motif, sandwiching a rerun of the main passages. Another enthralling song.

'Images (Chapter One)' (6.32) (J. Crichton, Sadler)
'Images' serves as a thematic and narrative introduction setting the first stage for the sci-fi story that Saga develop across multiple albums, focusing on futuristic, dystopian imagery. Jim Crichton explains that Einstein has been drawing his whole life, but the pictures get washed away by the rain. He knows he's about to die and at the end of 'Images', he does. Sung with immense feeling by Sadler, it's a poignant tale that evolves over the next 24 years. The song itself is in keeping with the forthcoming doom and it's a ballad with Chadd playing a beautiful, melancholic piano introduction. It's Sadler who plays the keyboard live. The feel is almost cinematic, with complex arrangements, including precise guitar layering and keyboard and bass phrases that weave together, each perfectly synchronised when combined. Sadler's vocal style is reflective of his choirboy roots and works well with neat harmonies (Chadd?). The vocals end midway through the song, leaving the rest to pick up the pace for the grand orchestral finale. An excellent acoustic version of the track appears on *Symmetry*.

'Hot To Cold' (5.01) (Sadler, P. Rochon)
A complete change of temperature and tempo from *Images,* beginning with a quirky keyboard intro and Negus bringing the rest of the band in with a perfectly executed press roll. He proceeds by not playing an obvious back beat as Jim Crichton's bass keeps 'running' in the background, maintaining the flow. The same beat continues throughout the verse (Sadler's lyrics), with alternating lines added by Chadd. The chorus is a more standard rousing repeat of the song's title, with 'Too hot to hold' added. The middle eight

follows the Saga rulebook with another bombastic instrumental rendition and Ian Crichton soloing underneath. The chorus then fades to the end. A satisfying and likeable track.

'Mouse In A Maze' (5.44) (J. Crichton, Negus, Rochon)
A song that explores themes of confusion and entrapment. Gross reckons that the track was mixed eight times and they may well have spent 100 hours on this alone. He felt that it was a good track, but it could have been a 'gem'. Synthesisers play a prominent role in creating an almost claustrophobic atmosphere that reflects the 'trapped' theme. A vocal harmony forms the introduction, with Sadler belting out Jim Crichton's lyrics. There's a slight gap before some intricate twin passages from Chadd and Ian Crichton, executing more trademark Saga keys and guitar accenting, leading to the first verse. The instrumental bridge between verses is a highlight, driven by Crichton's simple but powerful riffing, allowing keyboard and bass to propel the song. The chorus – 'He's a mouse in a maze, with its so many ways but there's only one way to get out' – stomps along, with Negus tastefully filling in at the end of each line. Great song, terrific album.

Silent Knight (1980)

Personnel:
Michael Sadler: lead vocals, keyboards, bass guitar
Jim Crichton: bass guitar, Moog bass
Jim Gilmour: keyboards (Moogs), vocals, vocoder
Ian Crichton: acoustic and guitar
Steve Negus: drums, percussion
Arranged by Saga
Recorded at Phase One Studios, Toronto, Canada
Produced by Paul Gross
Recording engineers: Alan Thorne and Mick Walsh
Remix engineer: Mark Wright
Album concept and design: Zoran Busic
Illustration by Tony Roberts, Young Artists, London, England
Running time: 37:44
Release date: November 1980
Label: Polydor Records
Highest chart places: CN: 42, US: did not chart, UK: did not chart

The 1970s have gone and so has Gregg Chadd, replaced by keyboard wizard, Jim (Daryl) Gilmour, who was 21 when he joined Saga just as *Images At Twilight* hit the shops. Jim was preparing to go back to university following an unsuccessful musical venture when he was called by Clive Corcoran, Saga's manager, who had heard Jim's band in one of their 'saloon recitals' and asked him to audition. He was successful. More details are in *Saga The Biography*. It was clear that Gilmour proved to be the missing ingredient, fitting in not only musically but personally, too. Gross: 'Jim was like a breath of fresh air. An amazing keyboardist who could also sing and compose at a highly accomplished level.'

Gross has fond memories of the final album of his trilogy, believing that this showed Saga at their best in terms of production and quality of songs, being particularly proud of 'Don't Be Late'.

Technically, there were more resources in the studio and this was the beginning of a great era of new recording equipment. Digital reverb, delays and a host of new processing gear were all eager to be used. Gross explained that the recording process hadn't changed much from the first two albums. The arrangements were always worked out beforehand and they would lay the drum track down first and build everything from that. Every track was painstakingly put in one after the other. 'In those days, we only had 24 tracks, but we virtually used every inch of tape. *Silent Knight* was mixed to a new half-inch tape format, which sounded bigger and punchier.' From the *Synopsis* EP, Paul Suter from *Sounds* on 8 November 1980 wrote:

> *Silent Knight* sees them maturing way beyond *Images At Twilight*, refining their cultured keyboard-orientated approach to give it much more bite than

before and putting the brake on the wilfulness that sometimes tended to fracture their songs a little too much in days gone by. They're still nowhere near conventional, though and their own development as a band now rules the likes of Genesis and Supertramp. If this album doesn't crack it for them, the next one will.

Matthias Mineur also observed that 'the album undeniably benefitted from the great euphoria amongst the musicians after two successful tours with Styx and Magnum'.

The album cover features an image of The Einstein Tower, situated in Potsdam, Germany. When Saga saw the artwork, Sadler immediately came up with the title *Silent Knight*. The LP was released in Canada in November 1980 and reached gold in May 1983.

In February 1981, Saga began another European tour, this time headlining, playing five shows in the UK, one each in the Netherlands, Switzerland and Denmark and 11 in Germany. Three albums' worth of excellent songs and much live experience ensured this was another successful and enjoyable outing. The bonus track on the 2002 CD is 'Don't Be Late' (Video Track).

'Don't Be Late (Chapter Two)' (6.04) (J. Crichton, Sadler, I. Crichton)
Following on from 'Images' (Chapter One), Jim Crichton explained that the deceased Einstein is taken to a place where people from another planet will put him in another body. Gross describes the track as...

> ...punchy, but it has a big, grand style that was very original. The layering of Moog tracks to create the orchestrated ending was something Jim Crichton strived for. Woven with Ian Crichton's soulful guitar, it makes a huge wall of sound to end the track. The song is a well-crafted masterpiece of ideas that, to me, is the early defining sound.

A rousing opener to album number three, the growth in confidence writing, performing and producing is evident. Saga have now found their feet in style and direction. The track doesn't immediately draw you in, but it was one of the band's most popular songs, appearing on the vast majority of all the live releases and compilations. Welcome, Jim Gilmour, an exceptional musician, with breadth and depth of skill and dexterity. Gilmour brings variety in his approach to the songs, heard immediately within this track, which musically and lyrically is a work of art. It's a relaxed pace throughout, even with the tempo changes. Grandiose keyboards feature most prominently, but the rest of the band are also in fine form and there's a lot to like about the structure and execution.

Swirling synths begin the adventure as a prelude to Sadler enthusiastically narrating the story so far across the verses and chorus, the latter being an atmospheric whispered call and response. Splitting these are short but highly entertaining instrumental passages with memorable lead phrasing. At 4.06, a monumental and bombastic orchestral passage is released, with dazzling displays of keyboard, guitar, bass and drum artistry. It's an amazing demonstration of musicality and this segment alone puts Saga right up there amongst their peers.

It's hard to believe that the song lasts for six minutes; it's over too quickly. It was released as a single with the B-side 'Time To Go', the accompanying video is a mock live affair and the band clearly enjoyed the experience.

'What's It Gonna Be?' (4:30) (J. Crichton, Sadler, I. Crichton, Negus, Gilmour)

It's full throttle for a track with a pop-rock feel, Negus displaying a pinpoint sixteenth-note application on the hi hats, one of his trademark chops to set the tempo. More observation-based lyrics from Jim Crichton, apparently concerning confrontation and accountability, come in the form of only two verses. It's a rollicking song, particularly during the choruses with sparse use of the vocoder, courtesy of Gilmour. It's a great bridge, too, with both Jim Crichton and Negus performing individual but complementary mini solos. Sadler questions 'Don't things look better in the night, to you' before Negus steps on the gas to pave the way for a short, impactful synth passage before the tempo pulls right back for the outro. Ian Crichton then steps forward to deliver an understated finale demonstrating his aptitude for melodic phrasing. Gilmour gets his first writing credit. This was released as a single with 'Compromise' as the B-side.

'Time To Go' (4:24) (Sadler, J. Crichton)

My favourite track on the album and one of my all-time favourite Saga songs. It slots in incredibly well within the album despite its more laid-back feel. It was to be our first wedding dance, but I forgot to bring the LP.

A joint composition by Crichton and Sadler, with lyrics by the latter, the theme revolves around contemplation, change and moving on. There are some great words with no obvious rhymes and you do wonder where the inspiration came from. It's beautifully written and performed in 3/4 time, although it's not that clear until you count it. Gilmour begins with tasteful piano arpeggios and lush synthesisers. There is some deft cymbal work by Negus prior to the first verse, the style being a soulful and heartfelt Sadler. The track flows through each passage effortlessly; the keyboards are magnificent throughout and the art of placing the accents is perfectly demonstrated by the rhythm section. Gilmour ends the track as it began. It's a pity that this doesn't feature live more, only appearing on *Live In Hamburg,* but it manifests magnificently on *Symmetry*.

'Compromise' (3:21) (Sadler, J. Crichton, I. Crichton, Negus, Gilmour)

A track written by the whole band, with lyrics by Sadler, who plays keyboards when it's performed live. Most memorable is the simple chorus chant of

'Compromise' in between the three verses, which deal with confusion, frustration and making choices: 'What'll it be this time'. The standout feature is the repeating instrumental segment interspersed with complex and experimental passages, all held firmly by Crichton's stomping bass. Gilmour then returns with a piano accompaniment over the leading refrain before Crichton lets rip with a short but intricate solo. A classic Saga ending full of pomp and energy, which was rightly deemed strong enough to be released as a single.

'(You've Got) Too Much To Lose (Chapter Seven)' (4:41) (J. Crichton, Sadler, Gilmour)

Crichton's thoughtful lyrics make up only two extended verses and a chorus that repeats the song title. Some lines in particular are reflective of the sci-fi themed cover artwork of a dark, foreboding landscape in keeping with the 'Chapters' storyline: 'And as the numbers grew, their swarm blackened his view'. The track is therefore dark with Gilmour's complex synthesiser opening gradually increasing the anxiety that morphs into the song's main motif, which is incredibly catchy. The verse features a strong bassline beneath Sadler's sprightly vocals and the chorus, although short in words, is anthemic and chantable. Similar to most tracks on the album, the tempo drops, then builds to a full-on keyboard assault and a smidgen of guitar solo ending with a chorus. The instrumental breaks are intricate, showcasing each member's technical proficiency. Mysteriously not favoured for live performance and only appears because it had to on *The Chapters Live*.

'Help Me Out' (5:52) (J. Crichton, Sadler, Negus)

Gross recalls how the band had worked almost all day to produce the clarinet sound at the end of the song using a synthesiser. After the recording, Gilmour casually mentioned that he could actually play the clarinet, something he'd also omitted to mention during his audition. After a brief, smooth synthesiser opening, Sadler delivers his conversational lyrics, where he chats and offers advice to a person who 'sits there like there's nothing wrong' and whose silence might be holding them back. Sadler's unique vocal style, combining clarity, precision and controlled intensity, is never better emphasised than here. The track has a lighter, more playful energy and as is Saga's nature, it is validated by the instrumental theme between verses, which is instantly recognisable when played again. The verses glide, but the chorus is more jittery with a punchy syncopation and the instrumental breaks ooze improvisation, wandering across different keyboard lead passages. When performed live, Jim Crichton will switch between bass and Moog for added dynamics. The song meanders to a fade ending, which somewhat diminishes its impact.

'Someone Should' (4:08) (Sadler, J. Crichton, Gilmour)

Whilst I might be a tad critical of the ending of the previous track, it does lay the foundation for 'Someone Should', which comes pounding straight in. I love this track and although it's not my all-time favourite Saga song, it's the one I play the most. It's instantly likeable and uplifting, summing up Saga during their Paul Gross era. Gilmour is the co-writer and his influence is now being felt through the execution of a monumental keyboard riff. The lyrics are courtesy of Sadler and could well have been another 'Chapter' if the 'Young Albert' referred to is indeed Mr Einstein, with 'Little Audrey' possibly being a sibling. If not, it's still entertaining stuff, with some interesting wordplay (rhyming 'senses' with 'fences') and concluding that 'Someone should tell them to go back, they're likely to forget where they are'. Musical highlights include the main motif, which is as good as they've done so far, the continuous keyboard riffing, the full-on synth assault, with impressive arrangements and the solid, uncomplicated rhythms. When performed live, the twin guitar keyboard solos are stunning. Sadler inadvertently sums up this track and the beauty of Saga in the last three words of the penultimate line in verse two: 'pomp and splendour'.

'Careful Where You Step' (4:22) (J. Crichton, Sadler)
A fast-paced, driving track with a memorable keyboard riff and some impressive duetting between the guitar and bass with masses of energy and rock-solid commitment. It's a popular live track, appearing on six live albums and all five DVDs, quite often opening the proceedings. It's got an instantly recognisable intro made up of a synth note held over menacing echo over 16ths on the hi hat, Negus lifting the foot to open it at just the right time to give it a distinctive groove. Gilmour produces another recognisable fanfare, laying the foundations for a stomping pulse during the verses. The track has military implications – 'landmine vision', 'secret weapons', 'there may be a mine under there' – complementing the marching beat. The track concludes with another set of clever instrumental passages, where everyone has a showcase moment. It's stirring stuff and a superb ending to a magnificent album. Live, it's impressive, too and one of the songs where the band revert to having three keyboard players, Crichton preferring the Korg MS2000. The track was released as a single with 'Compromise' on the flip and as a 12" single entitled 'Synopsis' with B-side 'How Long' and 'Take It Or Leave It'. The video was filmed at the same time as the one for 'Don't Be Late'.

Worlds Apart (1981)

Personnel:
Michael Sadler: lead vocals, keyboards
Jim Crichton: bass, keyboards
Jim Gilmour: lead keyboards, vocals, clarinet, lead vocal on 'No Regrets'
Ian Crichton: guitars
Steve Negus: drums, percussion, Simmons electronic drums
Recorded at The Farmyard, Little Chalfont, Buckinghamshire, England
Produced by Rupert Hine
Recording engineer: Stephen W. Taylor
Design and art direction: Shoot That Tiger!, London, England
Map illustration by Paul Cemmick
Photography by Collin Barker
Cover photo by David Kennedy
Running time: 43:37
Release date: 1 October 1981
Label: Maze Records, Portrait and Polydor
Highest chart places: CN: 22, US: 29, DE: 9, UK: did not chart

Saga's management were shifting focus to Europe, occupying an office in London, England, whilst Saga were keen to explore other production avenues. The band also moved to London with a working title of 'No Fixed Address' for the next release. Lavender Lodge, a house in Maidenhead, was acquired for writing and rehearsing.

Interviews for a producer took place and Rupert Hine was chosen. He had his own Farmyard Studios in Buckinghamshire, close to Saga's rehearsal space. Sadler and Jim Crichton were impressed by Hine's solo album *Immunity* and his unique sound processing and production techniques. Jim Crichton described him as 'one of the most imaginative producers he's ever worked with.'

Hine had just made an album with UK punk band The Members and was initially sceptical about working with a North American rock band, being 'unmoved' by the genre. However, he appreciated Saga's open-mindedness and was intrigued by what might manifest following his input and ideas. Hine stated that after their earlier albums, Saga felt they needed some fresh input, someone catalytic and on reflection felt that he and engineer Stephen Tayler brought a sharper, brighter, punchier mix, resisting the temptation of doing anything too extreme or bizarre.

Hine was forthright in telling the band where he thought they could improve, in particular, how Sadler could sound less like a 'choirboy'. Recording vocals whilst Sadler was still in bed for one track and placing him on top of a beam in the barn for another, were some of Hine's more unusual techniques, but they worked. Negus enjoyed the making of *Worlds Apart*, believing that it changed the chemistry of the band by bringing more objectivity. He considered it to be one of their best records. Hine was impressed enough with Negus, too and asked him to play on his *Waving Not Drowning* album.

In a feature in *Canadian Musician* in 1982, Sadler explained that this was the most prepared they'd ever been, with the nine songs chosen, each worked out well in advance and as a result, they recorded five backing tracks in just two days, which gave them more freedom to improve passages later. The album is also noted for the introduction of electronic drums, with Negus acquiring a set of Simmons, designed and built in England, with his help and already used by several pop and new romantic bands. Sadler:

> To say that making this record was a learning experience for each of us would be a gross understatement. We all agreed that together we had created something very special and this album was truly a game-changer for all of us in so many ways.

The album was released in Canada and Europe in October 1981 and was Saga's most successful long player, securing an appearance on the German *Rockpop In Concert* TV show, along with Meatloaf and Foreigner. They also played to a crowd in excess of 15,000 in Dortmund, watched by 27 million TV viewers in Germany and the bordering countries. In 1982, they won the German Gold Concert Ticket Award for outstanding sales and, in the same year, *Worlds Apart* received gold album status with 50,000 copies sold in Canada, followed by the Canadian Juno awards for the most promising band of 1981. Over 50,000 copies were also sold in Germany, resulting in another gold record.

The album was released by Portrait Records (sister label to Epic), with new cover work for the US, UK, Australia, South America and Japan. To maximise their first American record deal, support slots were secured with Jethro Tull, Billy Squire and Pat Benatar, followed by tours with Rush, UK and Styx. In *Kerrang!*'s February 1983 issue, Paul Sadler wrote:

> Reviewing *Worlds Apart*'s predecessor, I was moved to rashly suggest that 'if this one doesn't crack it, then the next one will.' Existing Saga fans will notice a distinct change in approach from the Paul Gross-produced era, with Rupert Hine placing more emphasis on the subtleties of the band, but the rock drive survives, as does the strong rhythmic base to their keyboard extravaganzas, making the appeal potentially universal.

The album achieved gold status in Canada in February 1982 and in Germany in August 1982. The bonus on the SPV 2002 CD is 'Wind Him Up' (Video Track).

'On The Loose' (4.10) (Saga)

Paul Sadler said to *Kerrang!* in February 1983:

'On The Loose' takes off like recorded racing through the clouds before breaking into clear sky with the dancing exuberance of its hook, the adroit drumming of Steve Negus pacing things along perfectly.

The Rupert Hine era begins with a track that is one of Saga's most popular songs, known by fans and recognised by others for its commerciality and radio play. It's a staple of all live performances because it's a phenomenally well-constructed, hook-filled tune. Hine's influences on the band are clear, resulting in a sleek and finely tuned pop-rock feel. The production is vastly different from that of Gross, being more mature and atmospheric, in line with the technological advancements in recording that accelerated during this period. It's the 1980s and Saga are in a different studio in a different country. 'On The Loose' maintains the hallmarks of Saga, tight arrangements, melodic hooks and synthesiser-guitar interplay, but up another rung or two. Written by the whole band, Sadler's lyrics are more wordy than previous offerings, expressing the achievement of freedom and control. After four bars of the opening refrain, the first verse thunders in with Sadler's purposeful and polished delivery – he's clearly benefited from Hine's direction – which is then followed immediately by a chorus, the main strength of the song. Gone are the relatively lengthy keyboard-driven instrumental breaks – the song has been designed to appeal to a wider audience. When performed live, it's phenomenal, particularly Sadler and Gilmour rocking away during the final section. Clearly a single, it got to number 22 in the Canadian charts and number 26 on *Billboard*, with 'Framed' as the B-side. It also featured on a double pack EP along with tracks from Loverboy's *Lucky Ones,* Journey's *Chain Reaction* and Aldo Nova's *Fantasy*, apparently an attempt by CBS to break North American bands in the UK. The video is on 'Silhouette'.

'Wind Him Up' (5.45) (Saga)

Another terrific track and like the first one, it became extremely popular with diehard fans and a significant chunk of the record-buying public across the globe. It's also an ever-present in Saga's live environment, being highly energetic with a strong, syncopated bassline and driving rhythm that creates an immediate sense of momentum. Jim Crichton tells the tale of Aldo, a compulsive gambler at the roulette table. A four-bar instrumental sequence opens before the first verse, followed by the bridge, featuring tight, controlled syncopated runs from Ian Crichton and Gilmour, with solid backing from Negus and Jim Crichton. The chorus is possibly Saga's most sing-along, with Sadler demonstrating his unmatched range and versatility. The quiet section has Jim Crichton on the Moog, with brother Ian's fabulous string picking, Negus uses the toms of his Simmons panning from speaker to speaker. Negus explained: 'We sound-processed the Simmons kit through a pitch-to-voltage regulator and that's what actually gave the white noise sound.' Sadler practically whispers the next chorus, accompanied by Gilmour's gentle synth. The track builds through another chorus to its conclusion. No extended solos, just a well-crafted pop-rock song and a great example of Saga's ability to create narrative-driven songs with memorable hooks. Being very radio-friendly, it was released as a single by both Maze and Portrait, with 'No Stranger' as the B-side, reaching number 64 on *Billboard*, popping up much later acoustically on *Symmetry*. The video sees the band in a casino, with Sadler having 'No luck today'. The track appeared on an obscure various artists compilation from CBS in 1983. 'The Rock Machine Still Turns You On' has Saga named first on the cover.

'Amnesia' (3.10) (Saga)
'Amnesia' combines a driving beat with an eerie, almost surreal keyboard line, embodying the lyrical theme of memory loss and disorientation: 'I live with amnesia, dancing with the shadows of my memory'. The line 'There's only total strangers everywhere I go' sums up what it must be like to lose your memory and not to recognise anyone. Interesting, too, because the word 'stranger' appears later in this album and several other times on future albums. Something for fans to watch out for. The hypnotic chorus skips along, with bass at the forefront, the keyboards appearing more in the instrumental section, before the track ends with an extended chorus. Paul Sadler commented on its 'commercial potential, churning and swirling textures, twisting into a magnificently appealing hook and the chance hit single in our synth-orientated charts is definitely there'. It did make it to 45 rpm, supported by 'Times Up'. The video features Gilmour trying to remember who he is, but eventually gets to the gig to join his mates on stage. It features a pink elephant, too!

'Framed' (5.40) (Saga)
The next Sadler composition is written in the first person and is sung with great conviction and angst in order to communicate the feeling of being wrongly convicted of a crime: 'Now my fate was their decision'. It follows on nicely from 'Amnesia', having the same feel and structure. The band revert to a signature instrumental break, interlocking synth and guitar, between verses and choruses. The choruses are very catchy, giving the song a more accessible feel without sacrificing complexity. At 2.40, the song drops to a quiet keyboard passage leading to a short section of stabs and agile bass and drum rhythmic exchanges. The tempo increases with Negus and Crichton powering through, allowing Ian Crichton and Gilmour to alternate solos. The former takes over with a staggeringly good display of fretwork, his best on the album so far. Randomly, the track also appears on The 'Sounds' compilation album *Schizophrenia*, released in 1983 on vinyl and cassette alongside contemporaries Loverboy, Aerosmith and Buck Dharma.

'Time's Up' (4.15) (Saga)
Back to a recurring theme of 'time', we are presented with three thought-provoking verses, written in the first person, that outline a mundane life, clock watching and nothing particularly to look forward to: 'Time's up you've been wishing your life away'. The music matches the sentiment perfectly; it's the ballad of the album and proof that Saga are also skilled in the melancholic. Keyboards and just electronic toms (no back beat required) set the smooth and ambient tone throughout. They're matched perfectly by Sadler's expressive vocals and Crichton's Moog undercurrents elegantly played during the quiet passage. The song has a dreamy quality and progresses from verse to chorus smoothly. The first line of the chorus, the track title, is beautifully sung by Penny Crichton. It's a unique offering and was released as a single with the B-side 'Amnesia'.

'The Interview' (3.50) (Sadler, J. Crichton)
In Paul Sadler's review of the album in *Kerrang!,* he picked out this track for the drums as much as anything else: 'Steve Negus thuds along magnificently as the song grows in warmth and texture.' It's an engaging start as the sequenced synth builds up briefly before the first verse is upon us. Four lines are sung before a Negus expansive fill picks up the story of a person who has come to the end of the road and is about to be replaced, but won't accept it: 'Don't you think it's time we had a younger face' ... 'How long do you think you'll last living with continuous past'. There's a lengthy bridge before the next verse, a clever arrangement with keyboards providing orchestral colour and more booming toms. Most of the instruments drop out during the chorus to allow Sadler to emphasise 'Tell me why you can't let go'. A carefully crafted and engaging song, with no particularly defining moments, though the hook is memorable.

'No Regrets (Chapter Five)' (4.41) (J. Crichton, Sadler)
A landmark track featuring Gilmour on lead vocals for the very first time and it's a lullaby. Throughout Saga's career, he has sung lead a few more times, often one track per album. He's been handed the excellent lyrics of Jim Crichton to sing the fifth instalment of the 'Chapters' saga. Gilmour sings softly with plenty of emotion, much needed for 'No Regrets'. The words have a nostalgic, moving quality about the potential decline of humanity and musically, this is also a Gilmour showpiece, utilising his expert touch and dexterity not just on keyboards but on clarinet, too. The perfect song to add a touch of woodwind for rich, warm and mellow tones. Two verses and a one-line chorus launch a new horizon for Saga and overall, this is a beautiful, introspective piece that adds depth and allows the listener a moment of calm amid the album's high energy. This was also a great live number, sometimes giving the band a rest whilst Gilmour performed solo. It got the acoustic treatment on *Symmetry*.

'Conversations' (4.44) (Saga)
Humour abounds in this 'instrumental', their first committed to vinyl, with just one lyric – 'Whadayawanna talk about' – and a repeating pattern of the effects-laden word 'Conversations'. They are no strangers to extended prog-themed instrumental sections, but to dedicate an entire song to the medium is, for Saga, experimental and innovative, emphasising their technical prowess and ability to handle complex, symphonic arrangements. Several background conversations introduce the track, leading to a layered combination of synthesiser and piano sequences that create shifting rhythmic patterns, alternating between pulsing ostinatos and broader harmonic swells, as the track progresses. Behind the kit, Negus is equally dynamic, with tight, controlled grooves and powerful, well-placed fills and Jim Crichton's bass provides melodic yet supportive lines that lock in closely with the kick drum. Ian Crichton adds further texture with carefully positioned harmonics and crisp rhythmic phrasing, with a touch of restraint to enhance but not dominate the mix. The result is an energetic, uplifting piece characterised by frequent changes in tempo and intensity. Disappointingly, this was not selected for live airings, only appearing on *Worlds Apart Revisited*.

'No Stranger (Chapter Eight)' (7.04) (J. Crichton, Sadler)
The album closes with another mightily significant song. It's the longest track on the album and it's the last 'Chapter' (for now). It's my favourite ever Saga song. Jim Crichton's lyrics are sublime, describing the ending of the first phase of the story. The protagonist becomes more self-reliant and is preparing for the next journey and includes the classic lines 'It wasn't long ago, so very long ago, I was one of your kind' and 'Maybe I'll be back in some other way'. The track has a slow build, atmospheric synth chords and a mysterious syncopated looped rhythm, with a gently played motif, the second most recognisable in the song. There's a continuous staccato piano stabs to 2.14, then bam! One of the simplest but most powerful guitar riffs in Saga's portfolio. It's a grandiose masterpiece that forms the background to the verse, which Sadler sings with heaps of conviction from the heart and the soul. Following the second chorus, Ian Crichton's stunning guitar solo incorporates tastefully blended shredding and expressive melodic lines; it's phenomenal and over too quickly. After another verse and chorus, the song decreases to what appears to be the end, only for a hushed piano to reintroduce the final verse, almost spoken by Sadler, with acoustic guitar added to the accompaniment. A true gem and Paul Sadler of *Kerrang!* agreed: "No Stranger' presents the album's most aggressive moments with a dynamic guitar pattern powering it relentlessly along.' It could and should have been a single in its own right, but at least it could be heard in jukeboxes across Canada and Europe as a B-side to 'Wind Him Up'. Also brilliant live with Sadler on bass guitar.

Heads Or Tails (1983)

Personnel:
Michael Sadler: lead vocal and keyboards
Jim Crichton: bass guitar and keyboard
Jim Gilmour: lead keyboards, vocals, sax
Ian Crichton: guitar
Steve Negus: drums, percussion, electronic percussion
Recorded at The Farmyard, Little Chalfont, Buckinghamshire, England
Produced by Rupert Hine
Recording engineer: Stephen W. Taylor
Art Direction and design: Spencer Drate and Judith Salavetz
Inner sleeve photo by Larry Williams
Front and back illustration by Stephen Burke
Running time: 40:01
Release date: 1 September 1983
Label: Maze Records and Portrait
Highest chart places: CN: 17, US: 92, DE: 3, UK: did not chart

Worlds Apart was a huge success, as was the subsequent tour, resulting in the live recording *In Transit*, released in 1982. For the follow-up, Rupert Hine was reinstalled at Farmyard Studios and in April 1983, the process began. Due to tour pressures, *Heads Or Tails* was recorded in just six weeks, not affording the band, producer, or engineer the same amount of time to 'think, plan and cogitate'. Sadler:

> We'd just returned from a very long and exhausting tour and really needed a break. But we decided to concentrate on writing new songs as quickly as possible, return to the studio and record *Heads Or Tails* to catch the momentum of the tour. Looking back, a little more rest and recuperation probably wouldn't have gone amiss.

The album received great reviews in Europe, but it was a mystery why the US didn't embrace it as they had with *Worlds Apart*, which had sold ten times more than *Silent Knight*. Hine:

> Before we started recording, we had intense discussions about whether it would be better to continue on a familiar path or whether we shouldn't perhaps take a little risk and try something new. Should the new material be more progressive and ambitious, or follow the request of numerous radio stations to come up with more of those highly popular, catchy, straightforward Saga numbers? The band and I agreed that we should go for the happy medium.

The album and its singles didn't get sufficient radio play to enthuse promoters in the US, so the focus on subsequent tours switched to Europe, mainly

Germany, rather than following the tried and tested path of supporting acts across North America. A US newspaper article in 1983 recognised an issue:

> What can you do when you are creators of a major hit album (*Worlds Apart*) but can't tour in support of sales because there is simply no one else going out on the road at the present time? This is the dilemma facing Saga, which is presently storming North American charts with their new album *Heads Or Tails*, but can't find a suitable act to accompany. Saga were still selling out venues across Europe, selling more than 200,000 copies of the new album in West Germany alone, reaching number three on their album charts, beaten only by Genesis (*Genesis*) and *Flashdance*.

On 14 February 1982, Saga became the first Canadian band to perform behind the Iron Curtain, playing to 10,000 fans in Budapest. The following year, they embarked on the *Heads Or Tails* tour, their longest and most ambitious to date. The shows were impressive with a spectacular light wall providing a visual delight for the audience, but at a high cost to the band. They eventually tried to sell it to the British band Magnum. Jim Crichton: 'The video wall, with its countless panels, cables, plugs and screws, ate up a bigger production budget than we really had, but people fondly remember that spectacular stage show to this day.'

Paul Suter, writing in *Kerrang!* in November 1983, reviewed the album:

> Two and a half years ago, I stood mesmerised at a Saga show in Puerto Rico; the experience of witnessing 15,000 people going crazy over a band that meant sod all virtually everywhere else was something to be savoured. Now, the world is catching up with those unlikely visionaries, the band's first US release achieving top 30 status earlier this year and in *Heads Or Tails*, they've come up with an album to bring the rest of the world in line. The band's ability to turn basic rock into something refreshingly different is continually revealed. Every number is totally individual and a review could constitute a paragraph on each ... Go out and buy the record and let it speak for itself.

The original vinyl release came with a free single, 'recorded live and previously unavailable in the UK'. It's 'Careful Where You Step' and 'Don't Be Late' from *In Transit*. The album reached gold in the US in July 1983. The SPV 2003 and earMusic 2021 reissues had an extended version of 'Catwalk' as a bonus

'The Flyer' (3.41) (J. Crichton, Sadler)

A song written and recorded with radio play in mind, it's one of Saga's more well-known songs. Although still a Rupert Hines production, it's different from anything on *Worlds Apart*, being a more upbeat, straight-ahead pop rocker, with a catchy chorus and a set of clever lyrics addressing ambition and single-mindedness. The production is pristine with Steve Negus still caressing the Simmons and Ian Crichton cleverly inserting the occasional tasteful flourish. It's got a standard structure of two verses, two choruses, a middle eight and a stellar guitar solo. A superb song that achieved its aim of shifting singles and promoting the album being released in various formats, as a single with B-side 'Conversations' and a 12" with the song as an 'extended rock mix' and a 'club version' with 'The Writing' remix. The video sees Sadler running through a minefield.

'Cat Walk' (4.25) (J. Crichton, Gilmour, I. Crichton)
Ian Crichton discussed 'Cat Walk' with *Prog* magazine journalist Rich Wilson, featured in the August 2014 issue. He recalled that the band were under pressure from their label to score another hit following 'On The Loose'. The track is significantly different in style and structure from the previous track, with a slower tempo, a funky groove and shorter vocal lines delivered by Sadler. Jim Crichton's lyrics suggest a metaphor for caution and the idea of walking a fine line, so nothing to do with the fashion industry. Gilmour starts with a smooth, ringing synth joined by Negus and then Ian Crichton with raw, distorted guitar phrasing settling into the main riff. Sadler sings with conviction over a throbbing bassline that defines the song's sleek and strutting feel and the chorus has a similar swaggering groove, but sparser. Saga reintroduce different instrumental segments between verses, featuring layered keyboards and an all-too-brief Crichton guitar solo, recorded in one take. It's a long outro with Sadler repeating 'he's got a catwalk' multiple times whilst the rest of the band add intricate touches along the way. It's another satisfying track with lots of small embellishments and technical depth. It was released as a single with 'Social Orphan' on the B-side and a video was filmed at Piccadilly Circus, London, with a leopard.

'The Sound Of Strangers' (4.08) (J. Crichton, Sadler, Gilmour, Crichton, Negus)
Michael Sadler's lyrics revolve around the theme of building confidence and being more decisive: 'Oh, the sound of strangers doesn't scare me any more', the recurring stanza being 'no more'. The track is also interesting musically as it sets a different cadence, being punchier and more spacious and atmospheric than previous offerings, the flow created by the open hi-hat rhythm and subtle snare fills during the verse. The chorus incorporates tight, immaculate harmonies on 'Clawing at the door' and 'Doesn't scare me any more'. The interlude features some clever call-and-response exchanges between each musician.

'The Writing' (4.12) (J. Crichton, Sadler)
More insightful lyrics by Jim Crichton this time about visiting a psychic – 'She looked down at my palm', 'her eyes could see the future', 'the clouds are clearing away, this losing streak will end today' – the message here is of hope

and positivity. A strident piano intro, tense and dramatic, leads into the first two verses, forcefully sung by Sadler. The chorus is more flowing and sing-along, with 'The writing is on the wall, those words will change it all'. The instrumental passages have the piano motif from the intro at the fore, reinforced by the guitar mirroring the rhythmic stabs of the bass and drums. The track accelerates at 3.27 with a fast roll across the kit and a lively finale crying out for a Crichton solo with dexterous taps and bends aplenty. Super song, but concert-wise, it only appears on *Heads Or Tails Live*, with Rob Moretti handling the vocals.

'Intermission' (5.27) (J. Crichton, Sadler, I. Crichton)
Side one closes with a slower, moody, atmospheric offering that's shorter on words (by Sadler) but still profound and interesting, with the theme being the passing of time and the changes that ensue as a result. 'I fall inside, reflecting eyes, dissolve in time' captures a quiet, meditative moment. The haunting melody matches the melancholic theme. The tension is created through the song's ebb and flow, executed by Gilmour's sustained chord patterns and Negus's gentle, alternating tom and snare beats. This continues throughout the first verse, Sadler providing just the right depth of expression and breath control. It's an exquisite vocal delivery. The instrumental sequence also maintains the song's core melody, allowing Ian Crichton a delicate and expressive solo, one of the highlights of a soothing and hypnotic song

'Social Orphan' (3.23) (J. Crichton, Sadler)
This fast-paced, full-on hard rock offering provides a lively and refreshing opening at 146 bpm, accentuated by keyboard stabs. The verses maintain the same tempo, as do the choruses, with some neat bass trickery following each line and complementary synthesiser placements. The Crichton duo take over during the instrumental sequence at 2.47, with Jim providing a solid but smooth walking bassline and Ian's trademark solo with a small, cheeky shredding demonstration. Michael Sadler's protagonist calls himself a social orphan, a person alienated from the mainstream, but willing to challenge it by being 'caught up in the game' and 'caught in the thrill of the chase', with the driving rhythm and tension created in the song perfectly matching the idea of being chased. It's another impressive track, with an energetic chorus and great musicianship in a pop-rock vein, which would have done reasonably well as a single, being powerful enough and short enough for radio play.

'The Vendetta (Still Helpless)' (3.44) (J. Crichton, Sadler, Gilmour, I. Crichton)
Written in the first person by Sadler, his protagonist feels trapped, imprisoned and 'helpless' as a result of the dominance of another. The final verse indicates regrettable revenge: 'It suddenly seems so calm ... What are we

supposed to do with all this new found freedom'. Musically, the song is tight and intricate with some impressive guitar and synth combinations. The song is dominated by a quirky, syncopated piano arpeggio and a constant, steady beat. The instrumental break stomps along, foot to the floor, almost marching, until the change at 2.31 to a more steady pace and a short guitar solo, introducing that defining final verse to conclude the story. Perhaps not that popular within the ranks, as it wasn't chosen for any other live releases, just appearing on *Heads Or Tails Live*.

'Scratching The Surface' (5.15) (Gilmour, J. Crichton)
Gilmour grasps lead vocal and lyrical duties with a song he penned with Jim Crichton. 'It's about television and being sucked into the media', explained Gilmore, who also thought it to be his finest moment. It was a single, selling reasonably well and became a crowd favourite during its multitude of live performances, where sometimes Gilmour goes solo. His open playing style is infectious and his clapping along to the instrumental section, on stage, is unforgettable. Gilmour's singing style is vastly different from Sadler's, but they do complement each other well, as evidenced in the earworm chorus. Held chords, synth loops and playful electronic toms adorn the verses. The choruses are also in 4/4 but with all the accents just placed on two and four, which gives a fragmented electronica feel. Enter Ian Crichton and one of his finest moments on the album – an extended guitar solo that demonstrates his skill. The single is accompanied by 'The Vedetta' and got to number 45 in Canada, helped by the video recorded in the Bahamas.

'The Pitchman' (5.38) (J. Crichton, Sadler, I. Crichton, Gilmour, Negus)
The perfect track to close out the album with energy and a sense of urgency. There are various definitions of a pitchman, but looking at Jim Crichton's lyrics, I'd say the nearest is from Collins: 'an itinerant vendor of small wares that are usually carried in a case with collapsible legs, allowing it to be set up or removed quickly', a typical product being jewellery ('Can you make it sparkle; can you make it shine'). Crichton's tale transitions between the buyer (mainly) and the seller, the former pleading for a fair deal. The track serves as a summary of the album's musical identity, combining the layered keyboards, dynamic rhythm shifts, melodic hooks and polished production that feature throughout the album. The first passage has some terrifically complex interaction between guitar and keyboards. It has a funky groove and the vocals are assured and defiant. From 2.13, it's instrumental/solo time and all take advantage. There are three distinct segments: a terrific guitar and keyboard solo; at 3.31, over a conversation in the distance, a series of precise single stroke rolls on the snare drum, tightly matched by the other instruments; then at 4.20, an express increase in tempo, pace and intensity with breathtaking rapid guitar and synth soloing and fast drum and bass theatrics to an eventual fade out ending. An exhilarating track to conclude a super album.

Bonus Track

'Cat Walk' (Unabridged) 7:44 (J. Crichton, Gilmour, I. Crichton)

Similar to the original, but with even more repetition of 'he on a catwalk, he's got a catwalk' and an extremely long solo from Ian Crichton exhibiting his full technical range.

Behaviour (1985)

Personnel:
Michael Sadler: lead vocal and keyboards
Jim Crichton: bass guitar and keyboards
Jim Gilmour: lead keyboards
Ian Crichton: guitar
Steve Negus: drums, percussion, electronic percussion
Sharon Benson: vocals on 'What Do I Know?'
Recorded at Compass Point Studios, Nassau, Bahamas, Powerplay Recording Studios, Zurich, Union Studios, Munich
Produced by Saga and Peter Walsh
Engineered by Peter Walsh
Sleeve design: Studio Convertino, Milan
Photographer: Fred Ereissing
Running time: 45:23
Release date: August 1985
Label: Maze Records and Portrait
Highest chart places: CN: 39, US: 87, DE: 2, UK: Did not chart

Saga produced demos of 11 songs whilst rehearsing at Compass Point Studio in the Bahamas from July to November 1984. They then moved to Zurich and Munich, writing two more songs before completing *Behaviour*. The whole process was felt to be challenging and expensive, resulting in different feelings and thoughts within the band about the merits of the location, the studio, the recording process and the songs. The album was released in July 1985 under a new label, BMG Ariola in Europe, Portrait in the UK and US and Maze (Bonaire) in Canada.

Reflecting on *Behaviour*, Sadler explained to Paul Suter of *Kerrang!* that *Behaviour* was a more straightforward album than *Heads Or Tails*, especially lyrically: 'It's the first time I've ever used 'love' in a lyric, which I swore I'd never do.'

The album was different from what had gone before, with a totally new style. It was the 1980s and a shift towards a more AOR and American commerciality; thus, the production had more style and gloss, transitioning into the realms of pop. Jim Crichton told Ammerlaan in *Saga The Biography:*

> I don't like *Behaviour*; I don't like the way we made the album; the band were coming apart at the seams. We were heavily in debt and it wasn't possible to keep working and living in the Bahamas – it was just stupid.

Ian Crichton concurred: 'In 1983, we moved to the Bahamas, where time slows down a lot. Writing this record there was inspiring but also distracting because of the beautiful environment.' Prior to the recording of the album, the band had an exhausting but successful few months behind them. *Heads*

Or Tails had sold reasonably well thanks to the single release of *The Flyer* and the extensive and expensive worldwide tour, but the band still felt that they should have spent more time in preparation and production. In interviews with Martin Popoff in 2002 and 2012, Sadler revealed:

> I still had a soft spot for the recording. I very much like *Behaviour*. There's just a feeling on that CD, something very special for me doing that record, the whole feel of that record. I was just in a very good headspace. I like the sound of the record, I like my vocal performance and when I hear it, I get that feeling back again of wherever I was at then. I like the songs and I think it's a good-sounding record.

The album reached number two on the German charts, but didn't perform as well in other territories. 'Misbehaviour' (Live) (Video Track) was the bonus on the SPV 2002 CD reissue.

'Listen To Your Heart' (3.51) (J. Crichton, Sadler, I. Crichton, Negus, Gilmour)
The music industry has moved on and so have Saga. This is a new era, a new studio and the band taking care of the production, the songwriting and approach to arrangements have also changed. This opening radio-friendly track is sentimental: 'Just look into my eyes, I'll always care for you'. The opening moments consist of haunting 'ohhh's from Sadler and swirling keys before the track intuitively grows, with a solid bass and a simple but effective guitar line over the verse. This tempo continues to the chorus, which incorporates harmonies to highlight Sadler's emotional delivery. The line 'Listen to your heart' and extracts from the chorus are repeated over a series of effects before a fade to the end. The production is strong, the playing and singing are exceptional and it's a well-constructed track, but very different from what's gone before. It's of its day and designed to have more mass appeal and thus was released as a single, reaching number 57 in Canada.

'Take A Chance' (3.50) (J. Crichton, Gilmour)
Written by the two Jim's with Crichton's lyrics. It's more up-tempo, but not unlike its predecessor, this has airwaves potential appealing to a wider market. 'I can see by the look in your eyes you're searching your heart once again', Sadler begins. A jaunty drum and bass intro for four bars heralds in the first verse, with echoed vocals being slightly down in the mix. The verse and choruses have the same groove, with a short instrumental sequence at 1.23. Crichton's sumptuous bass carries the song into the next verse. The main musical break consists of whispers, 'ad hoc' drum rolls, expressive guitar hooks, complementary free-flowing keyboard phrasing and that irresistible bass. It ends with a fairly long fade-out of the chorus. It was released as a

single by Polydor and it's the only track from *Behaviour* that made it on any live release: *Detours* and *So Good So Far*.

'What Do I Know' (3.37) (J. Crichton, Gilmour)
The tone and pace drop with this ballad, dealing with the possible breakup of a relationship: 'You were once my vice, now you're just like ice'. The song has an eerie sense through the use of a slow, drifting tempo, creative reverb-based ambient effects and the electronic drums. A simple piano intro, with Sharon Benson's beautiful voice, leads into the verse, with Sadler also singing soulfully. Benson emerges later during the break, delivering a stunning 'thinking about you', which ascends the track as does Crichton's skilfully created, flowing and imaginative guitar solo. It's masterful. The track concludes with more of Benson's soaring vocals and Sadler ad-libbing. Released as a single with 'Here I Am', the video sees the band in mock rehearsal and Sadler out and about with a young lady.

'Misbehaviour' (4.02) (J. Crichton, Sadler, I. Crichton, Negus, Gilmour)
The album's standout track is a full-band composition, with excellent emotive words by Sadler. He's mastered the art of writing in the first person, initially expressing the character's feelings, then transitioning to the other's point of view: 'But all this misbehaving is just what we need tonight'. One of the more energetic tracks on the album, the song has a steady groove set by the opening guitar riff, with just enough reverb and keyboard phrasing. Verse and chorus maintain a similar pace, but again Negus places the snare beat just on the count of four of the chorus to provide added space and dynamics to differentiate it more from the verse. A short, tasteful, mid-song Ian Crichton solo, which is impressive, introduces the next verse before another chorus. It was released as a single with 'You And The Night'.

'Nine Lives Of Miss Midi' (1.16) (Gilmour, Negus)
A track written purely by Gilmour and Negus and they were to collaborate much more in the future. It's a brief but pleasant instrumental, being four bars of ambient synth pads and sparse but effective melodic keyboard fragments, creating a calm and pleasant listening experience.

'You And The Night' (5.15) (J. Crichton, Sadler)
Side one closes with another ballad, the mood having been perfectly set by the previous song. Sadler himself described this to *Kerrang!*'s Paul Suter as 'one of the most emotional ballads of our career.' He supplies the lyrics, which outline the desire and need to be loved. A synthesiser swells over a legato piano effect, easing gently into the verse with a lone Sadler tenderly singing the evocative melody. The band unite for the next verse but keep the dynamics low, the electronic kit being a perfect choice to maintain the texture. Crichton's solo matches the delicacy of the vocal's sentiment with

each note carefully selected and executed. The chorus is repeated, drawing the song to its conclusion as the instruments gradually dissolve.

'Out Of The Shadows' (4.44) (Sadler, J. Crichton)
This track brings an edge back to the album with darker tones and more prominent guitar riffing. We're greeted by synthesiser, piano and syncopated drum beats, complemented by occasional frills from both Ian Crichton and Gilmour. It's a pleasant verse and chorus with a vigorous bass drum pattern, tom flourishes and echoed vocals. The bridge consists of staccato keyboards over a synth chord pattern, joined by a well-placed soulful guitar solo, then background riffing from Crichton, accompanying the main melody. Possibly one of the weaker tracks on the album, it does need more memorable passages and to be honest, the fadeouts are getting a bit tiresome.

'Easy Way Out' (3.56) (Gilmour, Sadler, I. Crichton, Negus, J. Crichton)
We're back to familiar territory with a rocky opening stanza featuring a crisp guitar riff for four bars and a super snare fill, repeated during the track, welcoming the verse. A soulful Sadler dominates the song with a forceful vocal display throughout, with Crichton's powerful guitar motif and Negus's snare attack also adding additional flavour. The chorus also rocks along, accentuated by precise riffing between the vocal lines and a driving four on the floor bass drum. It's a pleasant enough song without any particularly outstanding moments, but it's well-structured with some intelligent lyrics, again covering romance, emotional misalignment and the fear of loss.

'Promises' (4.10) (Sadler, J. Crichton, Gilmour)
The track follows a similar formula to most of those that have gone before, although with a slower tempo and finely placed musical embellishments by each player. An earnest Sadler delivers the words: 'She never makes commitments', 'She always tells me lies' and in the chorus, 'But when I hear those empty promises, I see through her disguise'. The lyrics on Behaviour are generally more direct and easier to interpret than on earlier releases, focusing less on abstract, conceptual themes and storytelling and more on personal emotions, relationships and individual perspectives. This track is laid back, cool, smooth and tranquil, with a wistful guitar lead providing one of the song's two main motifs, the sparking synth pattern supplying the other. Both are low-key but essential. There's no surprise how the song ends, but we are treated to another finely polished guitar solo.

'Here I Am' (3.56) (Sadler, J. Crichton, Gilmour)
Having been lulled by the previous tracks, 'Here I am' rocks. My second favourite track from this offering, with a different lyrical theme from Sadler, as his lyrics attempt to convince a person that they are in a worthless and possibly violent relationship and they should leave. Sadler's offering an

escape, 'here I am'. Crichton again provides the initial riff, the feel and tone being reflective of the rest of the album, introspective and slightly moody. The vocal melody has a sense of urgency, with Sadler hitting his full range with ease. The chorus is the best on the album; it stretches the emotions and has some lovely harmonies. Crichton again crosses the bridge with a technical, but expressive solo burst, which returns during the main instrumental sequence. The terrific ending features just vocals in an incredibly atmospheric final appeal: 'here I am, there you are'. It's an empowering and optimistic number.

'(Goodbye) Once Upon A Time' (6.36) (Sadler, J. Crichton, I. Crichton, Negus, Gilmour)
A track initially composed by Sadler on the piano whilst looking out across the Caribbean Sea. The final track on the album segways supremely from 'Here I am', with Gilmour's serene piano caressing the hair on the back of your neck for almost a minute. Fortunately, this refrain does return. 'As a child each day seemed to last forever' begins Sadler's story and it's one of his best in terms of imagery. It's simply about growing up and looking to the future, with the narrator describing each phase – the song is sung with passion. The chorus picks up the pace, but isn't ever fully unleashed. At 4.30, a change of direction harking back to the Saga of old, with short bursts and fast runs from guitar and keyboards, then a new sequence with Crichton's bass or Moog rhythmically grooving underneath all sorts of 'mayhem'. The rest of the song is a repeat of the chorus ad infinitum to a fade out. A song befitting the album's closure.

Wildest Dreams (1987)

Personnel:
Michael Sadler: vocals, keyboards
Jim Crichton: bass, keyboards, synthaxe
Ian Crichton: guitars, shadow midi guitar systems, synthaxe
Curt Cress: drums, percussion
Recorded at Goodnight LA studios, Los Angeles
Produced by Keith Olsen
Engineered by Brian Foraker
Front cover photo: Aaron Rapoport
Back cover photo: Penny Crichton
Art direction: Bob Defrin
Running time: 36:24
Release date: September 1987
Label: Atlantic
Highest chart places: CN: 77, DE: 18, US: did not chart, UK: did not chart

After the release of *Behaviour,* major frustrations emerged at the lack of success, particularly in the States, with disappointing sales, money running out due to extravagant spending on the back of *Worlds Apart*, the cost of living in the Bahamas and alleged financial mismanagement. This created internal tensions, causing the band to split into two: the Crichtons and Sadler on one side and Negus and Gilmore on the other.

On 2 April 1986, Negus and Gilmor dissatisfied with the way *Behaviour* had been written and recorded, played their last gig in Stockholm. In September 1986, an official announcement was made that the pair were leaving the band and they eventually formed the Gilmour Negus Project (GNP).

The other three began work on Saga's next album, *Wildest Dreams,* moving to Los Angeles to collaborate with producer Keith Olson at his Goodnight LA studios. German drum legend Curt Cress was recruited as the studio replacement for Negus.

Saga became part of the music technology transformation with the world's first digitally controlled analogue console and a state-of-the-art digital tape machine at their disposal, ensuring the album would be completely digitally recorded.

The band also managed to secure a much-improved distribution deal with Atlantic Records, but even that failed to spark interest in the US. Jim Crichton explained:

> Everyone was excited about the release, but the album did nothing; the kids liked the old songs better; they didn't want to hear us play simpler songs. If we could do *Wildest Dreams* again, I think Keith wouldn't change that much. He likes to keep things simple.

Ian Crichton, 'I think that the guitars came out on *Wildest Dreams* better, maybe because we didn't have a dedicated keyboard player. Keith is a guitar freak; he's one of my favourite producers. I liked what he did with Whitesnake. That big sound is great.'

Sadler: 'We didn't really have a plan of where our musical journey would take us, possibly that's why the recording turned out to be a little more pop-oriented than its predecessors, but we also featured strong progressive rock elements'.

Polydor issued the album on CD in 1994. It took another five months before they could tour due to Ian Crichton's broken hand. Cress was replaced by drummer Trevor Morrell (Wham, Kim Wilde) and Tim Moore (Nick Kershaw, Bee Gees) took over keyboard duties on tour. Gone are Negus and Gilmour and it is fascinating to hear what effect that has had. It's been two years since *Behaviour* and again it's a new studio, a new producer and another evolution in style. Sadler is now credited with keyboards in addition to vocals and both Crichton brothers play a synthaxe, 'a fretted, guitar-like MIDI controller that uses electronic synthesisers to produce sound.' It's an impressive-looking beast.

'Don't Put Out The Fire' (3.58) (Saga)

The opening track explores themes of desire, passion, a strong sense of personal motivation and emotional intensity, delivered through an energetic and engaging arrangement. It begins with brief, choppy synthesiser and percussive flourishes straight to the verse. Sadler's tone is similar to the previous record, soulful and mournful. The production sparkles with power and clarity. Olsen has provided a big sound and Crichton's guitar phrases in between the vocal lines and beyond are distinctive and a key element of the song, which has a steady, solid pace. Saga's bridges are always eventful and worth the wait and this one is no different. It's a deep and punchy synth (axe?) to dominate the passage, which includes short guitar and keyboard bursts. The end is similar to the beginning with a dead stop.

'Only Time Will Tell' (4.21) (Saga)

The track opens with a four-bar introduction, soon joined by Sadler's descriptive tale of loss and loneliness and I particularly like his reference to 'whatever happened to the friends we had, just a dusty picture on the shelf', returning to this theme in the final verse: 'Now where are you, are you dusting pictures too'. Keyboards emphasise the accenting during the verse, with guitar joining at the end of the lines, adding more power and expanding further on this phrasing during the choruses in classic Crichton style. Underneath, the bass bubbles along stylishly, changing only at the short bridge. It's a solid and enjoyable track with a great arrangement, combining atmospheric synthesisers with gentle guitar work, creating a soft soundscape. There's a heavier chorus towards the end of the track and plenty of embellishments from the entire band to keep the instrumental sections interesting. Malcolm Dome in *Prog* in October 2021 described it as an 'intelligent melodic pop song'. Released as a single, it was the album's biggest hit and a particular favourite in Canada, but even the MTV-friendly baseball-themed video only got it to number 93.

'Wildest Dreams' (4.58) (Saga)
The opening salvo consists of syncopated stabs and playful and improvised synthesiser effects. Sadler is in fine form, a master in the art of introspection, but from this minimalist approach to the lyrics, you can still identify that the song relates to holding onto hopes and desires. Cress's firecracker snare is high in the mix, but not to the detriment of the other instruments or Sadler's soaring vocals, particularly in the chorus. Ian Crichton also raises the game with another stellar solo between choruses and there's plenty of synthesiser counter-play beneath the main melody, supporting the transitions from light to shade. The song fades to its conclusion! It's one of the most accessible tracks on the album, representing Saga's attempt to reach a broader audience.

'Chase The Wind' (4.53) (Saga & Robin Prior)
Writing credits were also given to Robin Prior, a British songwriter who has also worked with Pendragon and Twelfth Night, which may well have been the main influence on this track. As much as any other track on the album, this one demonstrates the intricate production approach and the eagerness to use the full resources available in the studio. You get the idea in the first few seconds before it really gets going. Effects abound with a strummed guitar intro, percussive flourishes panned across the stereo spectrum, synth overtones and a solid bass to prepare for the vocals. Sadler doesn't disappoint with another expressive delivery. The conflict between romance and freedom appears to be the theme, which seems to be this and the previous album's main subject. The chorus maintains the same feel as the verse, a smooth mid-tempo groove and melodic pop-infused instrumentation. The composition is built around a recurring refrain that evolves throughout the song, with subtle changes in harmony, arrangement and intensity keeping each repetition fresh. This includes more impressive playing by the whole band, terrific soloing and an extended repeating chorus to hum to whilst turning the record over.

'We've Been Here Before' (4.45) (Saga & Curt Cress)
I can see the unintended irony as there is definitely a similar feel, structure and continuity to the whole album and that's not a bad thing, it's just that the band are now a three-piece without the creative input of Negus and Gilmore, which must have been challenging. However, Curt Cress, who has proved himself here to be an exceptional drummer, has slotted in extremely well, his style and chops perfectly suited to this recording. He brings energy and power but is also adept at subtlety and being totally supportive of others. This song is his only writing credit, but he'll be quite pleased, I'm sure, as this

track turns up on three of the live DVDs and umpteen live shows, more than any other track on *Wildest Dreams*. It's a shame that he wasn't there to perform it on stage, but Brian Doerner and Chris Sutherland did splendid jobs in their own way. It's got a spirited groove, minimal backing during the vocal sections, but still with a distinctive riff. Ian Crichton is afforded a lengthier solo and it's magnificent. See *Contact Live In Munich* for one of his most expressive leads.

'The Way Of The World' (4.18) (Saga)
My favourite track on the album opens with the synths bursting through with a sense of urgency created by bright arpeggios. The energy increases when guitar, drums and bass come thundering in. All that stops as Sadler, an 'octave' down from the last track, advises, 'You don't know who to be nice to, you gotta watch what you say and do', to the accompaniment of a signature, harmonically rich Crichton guitar phrase and a pounding bass drum pattern. The verse rocks along nicely, but it's the chorus, with a mysterious female voice and subsequent instrumental passage that really adds value. Bombastic, vibrant synths dominate with complementary expressive drumming, propelling the song! It's exciting stuff, even more so when appreciating Crichton's fast and intense soloing. There's the customary array of tempo changes, the bridge being a fine example in building a track back up and Sadler's vocal dynamics and harmonies are sublime, taking this song to another stratosphere. Welcome to the way of the world indeed.

'Angel' (4.20) (Saga)
This song has a similar opening to the previous track, with appealing short synth passages, but lesser in volume and intensity, allowing Sadler's more mellow and heartfelt tones to appear higher in the mix. This ballad's lyrical sentiment expresses longing and deep devotion, tempered by themes of hope, reassurance and emotional comfort – 'Only a fallen angel can set me free' – sung over lush synthesisers and gentle guitar phrasing. The majority of the track repeats the chorus, sung with heaps of passion and compelling harmonies and there's a sprinkling of a simple but extremely tasteful and beautifully executed guitar lead between the words. There are brief, low-key instrumental passages at 2.11 to provide a slight respite, but I'm not sure that it's absolutely necessary, as the song is strong enough without it. Released as a single through A&M, Jim Crichton thought that this should have been a hit, but it did become a mainstay of the live performances.

'Don't Look Down' (4.39) (Saga & Julia Downes)
Not to be confused with the 'Go West' song of the same name, which achieved significant success across the globe two years earlier, the Saga version is co-written by Julia Downes, a British songwriter who's also worked with Roger Daltrey, Meatloaf and Sheena Easton. The track has a quirky start

with deep bass tones (Moog?), playful sequenced synth punches and improvised drum fills and stabs. The verse is mid-tempo with a jerky feel due to the bass drum, guitar and Moog placements, but the chorus flows more with double-tracked vocals. During the instrumental section, the bass drum booms over a guitar ostinato and almost hidden 16th note hi-hats. At times, it all sounds a tad fragmented, making it less engaging and perhaps not the best album closer, but the final lines with just Sadler crooning 'you know you'll always have somebody' and a sustained synth work well. A popular live track, it was widely featured on subsequent tours.

The Beginner's Guide To Throwing Shapes (1989)

Personnel:
Michael Sadler: vocals, keyboards
Jim Crichton: bass, keyboards, synthaxe
Ian Crichton: guitars, synthaxe, banjo
Curt Cress: drums, percussion
Recorded and mixed at Picture This Studios, Los Angeles
Produced by Saga
Recording engineer: Jim Crichton
Mixing engineer: Brian Foraker
Drum recording engineer: Berthold Weindorf (drums recorded at Pilot Studios, Munich)
Album cover design and photographs by Penny Crichton
Art co-coordinator: Philippe Grabowski
Running time: 45:51
Release date: 30 October 1989
Label: Bonaire
Highest chart places: did not chart in Europe or North America

This marks the second album with the band as a trio and Curt Cress back behind the kit. This is a completely different offering than *Wildest*. That album is mainstream, commercial pop rock, polished and safe; this album is sharper and edgier, with more energy, offbeat riffs and more unusual phrasing and as such it definitely appeals more to me. It's a marvellous album demonstrating some great songwriting, arranging and playing and the production is glossy, clear and powerful. I always liked the completeness of the album and how the songs blend well together. It's not a concept album as such, but there seems to be a theme in the storytelling. However, it proved to be one of Saga's most underrated releases, perhaps due to a lack of publicity and/or the two missing members. As a result, the album had an all-time low in record sales, not charting in any territory, not even Germany. That's a real shame as it features some incredible guitar riffs and solos and displays Saga's wide range of styles, from classic rock, prog and ballad.

Saga toured Germany, Holland and Denmark, with Graham Lear (Santana) on drums and Richard Baker (Gino Vanelli, Santana), originally in Truck, on keyboards. The tours went well, but without Negus and Gilmour, it just wasn't the same. Sadler's thoughts on the album, included in the 2015 CD reissue liner notes:

> Once again, we enlisted the services of German drummer Curt Cress, who delivered another collection of fantastic performances. When you've only had some of the best playing with you, the only difference between them is what they bring to the table in terms of style, feel and interpretation and Curt's footprint is firmly embedded all over this record. I look back with

personal pride and would give it eight out of ten. On this album, I was starting to experiment with my approach to background harmonies. And I thought that Ian did a great job with all the solos on the album. He has an appealing melodic approach to soloing and there are a couple on this album that are definitely on my top ten list

The band didn't have a distribution partner at the time, so when released, the album was only available as an import, but it's still regarded by the Saga fans that I've spoken to as one of their very best. I agree, it's a fabulous record with a unique and extremely creative album cover. Jim Crichton explained in the 2021 reissue liner notes:

The expression 'throwing shapes' was frequently used on our 1988 European tour, with our production manager Chris Adamson coming up with unusual ideas to keep us amused. He screamed the word 'shape' and the entire band would hold a statue-like pose as long as they could. To create the front cover artwork, my wife, Penny, constructed a rear-lit silhouette backdrop in our garage. When someone came over to the house, she would quickly enlist them for a pose for the new album cover. We couldn't park our car in the garage for a year.

There are, in fact, 70 thrown shape images on the cover. Penny explains the process in more detail on her website. Malcolm Dome in *Prog* in October 2021 commented on the vinyl reissue:

The Beginners Guide To Throwing Shapes brought the band slightly back towards their prog roots and away from the influence of Atlantic. This was more in keeping with the early 1980s albums that had established their reputation, especially in Europe. Here, the band still dabbled in electronics, but for the most part, kept this side of things in check and both 'Giant' and 'Scarecrow' are reminiscent of what the band were doing on albums like *Images At Twilight*.

The album was reissued in 2003 on CD by SPV, remastered by Steve Negus with 'Framed (Live)' and as a digipak CD by earMusic in 2015 with a green cover and bonus tracks 'Wind Him Up' and 'The Flyer' live in Hamburg 2015. earMusic's vinyl reissue in 2021 included 'The Call (1991 Single)'.

'How Do I Look' (4.33) (Saga)

This is a vastly different proposition from *Wildest Dreams* and is much better. The past two years have seen the Crichton brothers and Sadler develop their songwriting and arranging abilities and as a collective, they've grasped the production reins, gaining full control over the sound of the record. This track is a great example, with its power, clarity, deft arrangements and excellent musicianship. We begin with some playful vocal conversations and a steady 41-second instrumental build-up before Ian Crichton's intricate and instantly appealing lead guitar line appears and is a constant throughout the track. Gone in the main are the romantic connotations and it's back to storytelling and personal reflections. This track's inference is slightly more obvious from its title; the protagonist wakes up disoriented, but a 'glance in the mirror' creates the thought 'I think I know who I'll have to be today' – the core message seems to be about the need to change personas to suit certain situations. Sadler also employs a technique he regularly utilises, improvising a vocal between the more formal chorus and/or verse lines. On this occasion, it works well. The full-on instrumental break is a Saga classic; the tempo drops, but the energy is still maintained and everyone is contributing, not competing. Solid and smooth bass foundations allow incredibly fast runs from Cress and Ian Crichton. For the latter, someone has moved the desk slider up a couple of notches, perhaps Ian himself, to ensure his outstanding fretwork cuts through. A brilliant start.

'Starting All Over' (4:01) (Saga)

A track that continues the evolution of this outstanding album and the stark difference in style from the previous offering. Two verses and four choruses form the main structure. It's a reflective theme about renewal, forgetting what's gone before and embracing what's to come. I particularly like the phrase, 'patience is a barricade', implying the need to just get on with it. After a stabbing synth opening, a brief piano trill heralds the vocals. Instantly recognisable is Curt Cress's funky and expressive groove and his distinctive bass drum pattern, never relying just on the one and three. This track is a great example of Sadler experimenting with harmonies, rich, melodic, tightly layered and almost orchestral. He declares this to be one of his favourite tracks in Saga's discography. I agree, this is a marvellous track, with some hallmark Saga, delivering complex yet accessible arrangements, including exceptional piano playing, riffs between verse lines and soulful soloing. The song starts to close down at 3.35 and is a useful palate cleanser for the next track.

'Shape' (5.10) (Saga)

The chaps were having fun in the studio, warming up and having a bit of banter, before realising that the 'tape' was still running, so they thought they might as well keep it in and use it as an opener. That's probably not true, but it does sound like it and it's not ineffective either. What's definitely planned is the motion created by the deep, thick and punchy synthesiser (Moog?), which provides the song's main melody. Ian Crichton's riff, following each line of the verse, is lighter and simpler than the chorus and I'd suggest the strongest one on the album. The song is built on high energy and soaring vocals from Sadler, who sings in a later chorus, 'I wear this disguise like a second skin', a nod to the story's meaning of identity, transformation and self-perception, with references to 'Frankenstein' and 'being some other guy'. The interlude features some exquisite dynamic phrasing and interaction with synth, Moog, or possibly synthaxe and the guitar is also very impressive. The chorus is used to fade out the track with Cress and Ian Crichton soloing over the top. Inspired is the reappearance of the clarinet, about time, too, with swirling, almost cinematic keyboard textures and angular guitar lines, making it one of the more challenging tracks on the album. An expert guide!

'Odd Man Out' (4.54) (Saga)
It's interesting to note the references to 'Strangers', 'Conversations' and the more obscure 'Half The Time', all titles of previous Saga songs. The latter is a song written and recorded during the *Images At Twilight* sessions, appearing later on the *Phase One* album. Saga always intrigue with their use of previous song titles. These introspective and emotionally charged lyrics look at life in the first person, exploring the feelings of alienation and possibly being misunderstood, themes covered by Sadler previously, so I'm guessing that these words are his, a particularly poignant line being 'I hear them whispering my name, am I the odd one out'. The introductory synth makes it apparent that this will be a quieter tune with a slower tempo and generous amounts of space. Sadler's tone is smooth and velvety and the acoustic solo is exceptional, perfectly complementing the ambience of the song. During the same passage, Crichton switches to electric to gracefully hold and bend the selected notes. Harmony vocals and synth rapidly dissipate to end the track.

'The Nineties' (4.16) (Saga)
Only one year to go and it will be 1990. Unbeknownst to Saga at the time, it would be a decade in which they would release five albums of new material, arguably their most creative and controversial period, with some very different and un-Saga-like music to discuss later. This interesting set of lyrics is perhaps more telling about their thoughts on the future. 'No way I'm ready for 2001, some things have got to change before that day comes'. In addition, the lyrics can be read from an environmentalist standpoint: 'I don't know how to patch a hole in the sky, I only know that we had better try'. No synth opening this time, just an acapella harmonised group chant of the first two lines of the chorus to begin proceedings before a bell rings, then the rest of the band come stampeding in guided by a crunchy guitar lick. The chorus is also chantable, with multiple voices adding to the texture. Alas, this would have been great live, had it been given the opportunity. The track belongs to Ian Crichton, who adorns it with rhythm and lead guitar flourishes perfectly placed during each passage. This was released as a single with the B-side 'How Do I Look'.

'Scarecrow' (4.20) (Saga)
This track uses a metaphor to seemingly explore themes of isolation and angst, building tension with its slower, more deliberate pace and having a

gothic cinematic vibe. Already referenced in track one, 'I hear the voice of the scarecrow calling me', it's now arrived and the tale is dark and scary, Sadler leaving us with the final two lines spoken: 'one of these days you'll wish you were dead, there's a scarecrow now lying under your bed'. It's got to be a Jim Crichton lyric, as this is the only track on the album that doesn't credit Sadler. Instrumentally, it reflects the words with a grungy, aggressive guitar ostinato that forms the main melody. Vocals are held back slightly in the mix and sung with overtone effects panned successfully. It's better with headphones. There's a minimalist vocal bridge between verse and chorus that adds more menace. The chorus itself is simple, with just an extension of the first syllable in 'Scarecrow'. The volume increases dramatically as Crichton approaches the end of his edgy solo, before another chorus and then a fade to the end of another excellent track.

'As I Am' (5.15) (Saga, Tim Moore)
Written by the trio with a contribution from American singer-songwriter Tim Moore. To me, this is the standout track which has speed, determination and a chorus to die for. It's catchy as hell, intuitive and memorable, with a terrific guitar riff. It's the album's heaviest track and would therefore perhaps have greater appeal to traditional Saga fans. It also incorporates awesome musicianship, with a shout-out to Jim Crichton for some inventive bass work. It's the synthesisers that begin the song, with a sprinkling of harsh reverb effects on the staccato piano before cymbal splashes bring in the verse, during which there is some astonishing interplay between guitar, keyboard and piano. The chorus is a more standard down-to-earth rock groove and the piano features on the break, with Cress pounding the floor with single beats, as Crichton's guitar solo evolves into a twin passage where it appears that he has either double-tracked, added another guitar, or has been joined by a colleague on keyboards. The track ends with a short fade-out, with the guitar riff still ringing in your ears.

'Waiting In The Wings' (4.55) (Saga)
This has a similar start to several other tracks, using tight keyboard phrasing to begin proceedings with powerful tom strikes to build the momentum. The keyboard-driven motif then powers straight in, which is replaced during the verse by the guitar's three-strum riff sequence at the end of each line. Vocals build in volume during each passage. The chorus doesn't flow directly from the verse but is preceded by a brief instrumental break. The chorus is catchy, likeable and head-shaking, the tempo dictated by pulsating bass runs and complementary linear bass drum. Sadler pounds out the words as he asserts that you're never alone and that there is always someone there for you and it's extremely convincing. At 2.38, the instrumental break is a lesson in complexity, one of the highlights of the album. It's a brilliant arrangement with incredible interaction between all, showcasing each musician's dexterity

and ability to effortlessly pop in and out of the different passages. Clearly, Ian Crichton visited his studio booth several times to excel with different lead arrangements. His fretwork is breathtaking, skilfully supported by the others, but it's his show.

'Giant' (7.10) (Saga)
The album's longest track is one inspired by the James Dean movie of the same name. Out comes the banjo again and an elderly voice to start the track with a 49-second narration introducing the story: 'Legend has it that one day a stranger rode into town', he begins. Cress's fabulous-sounding bass drum pounds away in fours, laying the foundation for the synthesiser to create the main melody, which is later joined by a similar guitar line. It's a potent mix. Sadler is controlled and relaxed as he continues the story, a reflective and emotional tale of feeling different and standing out from the rest. At 3.45, Sadler announces 'all change', at which point the pace turbo-charges for nearly a minute, allowing Ian Crichton to shred frantically. Following several repeats of the chorus, the banjo and a narrator return to conclude the story. This time, it's Ian (The Scottish Cowboy) McCorkle, an authentic nod to the Crichtons' Scottish heritage, explaining that the townsfolk did indeed listen to the stranger and 'take note'. He's gone now, but won't be forgotten. Sadler himself described the track perfectly in the 2015 CD reissue liner notes: 'The song has all the elements that make the Saga sound, including a banjo. It's all there, great musicianship, strong vocals and an absolutely killer guitar solo.' However, incredibly, not one track from *Beginners* featured on any subsequent live recordings, which is both a mystery and a disappointment.

Single
'The Call'
Released in 1991
Written and recorded to get airplay and have commercial impact, this is not a true reflection of the band by any stretch, but it's worth a punt. It doesn't sit comfortably with this album, or indeed any other Saga record, but it's pleasant enough. The track revolves around a shuffle rhythm with a chorus that you'll be singing for the rest of the day, but there's nothing remarkable from a writing or performing perspective. It didn't chart.

The Security Of Illusion (1993)

Personnel:
Michael Sadler: lead vocal
Jim Crichton: bass guitar
Jim Gilmour: keyboards
Ian Crichton: guitar
Steve Negus: drums, percussion
All other instruments: Jim Crichton
Recoded at Sound Image, Van Nuys, California
Recording engineers: Steve Negus (keyboards), Ian Crichton (guitars)
Produced by Saga
Mixed by Shy Baby
Art direction and design by Vivid Images (Ioannis, Liz Vap and C. Knippenburg)
Painting by Walter Gabrielson
Running time: 48:32
Release date: 27 January 1993
Label: Avalanche Records
Highest chart places: DE: 46, CN: did not chart, US: did not chart, UK: did not chart

Returning to Ammerlaan's biography, Saga were gigging in Germany with Kansas and Nazareth when their manager, Michael Ellis, spotted Jim Gilmore in the audience and persuaded him to come backstage. The story, as told by Gilmour, is featured on the 2002 *Silhouette* DVD and goes like this:

> I was in Munich and I knew the band were in town, so I decided to see them. I grew up with these guys; they are like brothers to me. Mike was shocked to see me, but he got me a backstage pass and asked me to see the band after the show. I didn't want to, I was too nervous, but he forced me. It was amazing; there were tears in people's eyes. But nobody really discussed the possibility of a reunion yet.

It wasn't until Sadler met Gilmore at a music fair in Frankfurt in 1992 that the reunion idea was mooted and soon the five discussed the feasibility of creating another album together. Negus admitted that the *Gilmour Negus Project* hadn't been as successful as they had hoped and the 'water was well under the bridge', so it made absolute sense. Not only was this the first album recorded with the original lineup since the split in 1987, but it was also the first album recorded at Jim Crichton's Sound Image Studio, located next to Keith Olson's Good Nite LA.

The reunion worked and they were back in the studio recording *The Security Of Illusion* in 1993. Gilmour stated that it was a great feeling when the album was finished, Negus adding that things had changed for the better; any disagreements didn't seem as important. The whole experience was more enjoyable than their previous album together. Ian Crichton agreed that this was a special record for Saga; he also felt that the new studio was 'awesome' with all recording options available, analogue and digital and multiple ambient rooms. 'Of all the Saga records, this one has the loudest guitar mix of all.'

The cover artwork was courtesy of artist Walter Gabrielson. Jim Crichton remembers going over to the warehouse in LA where Gabrielson kept his paintings to look for front covers and for something to spark an idea. 'When we came across the painting, *The Security Of Illusion*, the concept was born.'

Malcolm Dome in *Prog* in October 2021 wrote, 'everything about this album seems balanced and confident as the classic lineup flexed their muscles. It was as if the other three had suddenly rediscovered their mojo.'

Reissues of the album include SPV's 2003 CD with bonus 'The Security Of Illusion' (Acoustic Version). This also appears on the earMusic's 2021 vinyl reissue and their 2015 CD version, which also has 'Scratching The Surface' and 'Ice Nice' live in Munich.

It's been four years since the last album and the band are back together again. These were exciting times for Saga fans. The previous album was a cracker, but didn't shift as many units as it deserved. How had Saga evolved, individually and collectively?

'Entracte' (0.58) (Saga)

The opening track didn't give any clues. Entracte is an instrumental. Laughing, talking, an accordion, it's a party, it's a circus, it's atmospheric, it fades in and then fades out.

'Mind Over Matter' (4.35) (Saga)

Saga are producing again, with mixing by Shay Baby, in Jim Crichton's studio. As usual, the production is pristine, with everything recorded being easy to hear and appreciate; it's analogue-like, rich, full-sounding and layered with ambient textures. Ian Crichton's crunchy hook dominates the opening phrases and the verse melody with some powerful riffing. Steve Negus is back and so is the bell of the ride cymbal used sparingly but well. The natural volume is high, so watch your speakers and Sadler sounds like himself, perhaps a bit more casual to suit this track, but in fine voice, projecting each word precisely and coherently. The chorus is smooth with more extended phrasing and the short instrumental has Crichton showing off on rhythm and lead guitars, with some impressive 'acrobatics'. It's a great opening track, hard-hitting with strong riffs and a memorable chorus and it does follow on nicely from the previous album. So, not too much has changed, it would seem.

'Once Is Never Enough' (6.04) (Saga)

Jim Gilmour wasn't that distinctive on the opening tracks, but he is now with a gentle swirling ambient synthesiser, making full use of the stereo channels. A couple of tight single-stroke rolls on the snare bring in the eight-line verse, driven by an ongoing staggered rock-fused guitar riff. The first break sees Gilmour's alternating lines with Crichton, like they used to and Sadler increasing the temperature with more inflections in the chorus. 'Thrill of the chase, when you get what you want will that be enough'. Gilmour's back to add more texture to the instrumental sections and at 3.40, Crichton is given eight bars to provide the lead, of which he takes full advantage. As the track begins its countdown, Negus takes the opportunity to demonstrate some of his impressive chops, gliding around the kit. Malcolm Dome commented in *Prog* in October 2021: 'With its intricacies and instrumental vibrancy, this is old school Saga'. He's right and once isn't enough.

'Alone Again Tonight' (4.14) (Saga)
Lyrically, this is a strong and heartfelt love song capturing the despair of solitude, with Sadler crooning to what would appear to be his estranged partner, 'cause I know where we went wrong'. The rest of the band are in splendid supportive mode, keeping it laid back and relaxed throughout verses and choruses that merge effortlessly into each other with an immaculate keyboard refrain and the bass is sumptuous in tone and melody. There's no change of tempo and only subtle variance instrumentally for the chorus, mainly synth-based and Sadler accentuating the passion, 'I didn't mean to hurt you, I never meant to complicate your life'. We're treated to 36 second guitar solo, Ian Crichton maintaining the elegance of the song with a range of well-executed phrasing. Perhaps not the usual Saga fare, but it works well as a melancholic ballad, raw and emotionally charged.

'I'll Leave It In Your Hands' (4.38) (Saga)
We're in familiar territory with a moderate pace and a distinctive Saga side two opener. My fellow Sagaite, Rob and I had a saying we used when a new Saga album was released. We'd identify the tracks affectionately as 'Saga by numbers'. This is one of them. We're treated to Gilmour's chords at the start, then Negus adding tasteful tom stabs and Ian Crichton's simply initial guitar phase, all anchored expertly by Jim Crichton's smooth basslines. The first verse is sung beautifully by Sadler, who showcases his vocal range, the higher notes reached with ease and used expertly across both verse and chorus, which are seamlessly joined by Ian Crichton's quintessential heavy guitar riff. Other highlights include the guitar hook midway through the chorus, the song's complementary verse and chorus melodies, Sadler's soaring notes and Crichton's standout solo, venturing more to the bottom of the neck, then moving back up very fast indeed. This is a terrific song with a fantastic vocal bridge, 'I still have faith' and a staggeringly good instrumental passage.

'The Security Of Illusion' (5.40) (Saga)
The track opens with carefully plucked acoustic guitar harmonics before shifting into strummed chords that introduce the song's main melody to

accompany the vocals for the first verse, in which Sadler has clearance to express himself and is passionate and soulful, meaning every word. A gentle drum beat joins in on the chorus over an immersive keyboard quietly padding out the background.

This is very much a vocal track, with Sadler finding comfort in the 'Security of Illusion', which is repeated ad infinitum. The track features a mix of melodic hooks with minimal instrumentation, embodying the themes of deception and self-reflection that thread throughout the album. It's a relatively popular track, being only one of two songs from this album that make it onto a live release. It was also a single with 'Stand Up' as the B-side.

'Stand Up' (4.12) (Saga)

First up is a characteristic guitar riff from Crichton's very large book of his own classic riffs. It's simple, impressive and catchy and forms a large part of the track. It drops out at the verse, giving way to mainly a moderate drum and bass groove. The latter is also memorable, demanding that we 'Stand up, show this world what you are made of, keep the dream alive'. Midway through the instrumental break at 2.51, smooth, funky bass patterns dominate to lay the foundations for some playful guitar extracts before Crichton switches back to the introductory monster riff, then the anthemic chorus gently eases us out.

'Days Like These' (4.48) (Saga)

A vigorous bass marks the arrival of the track and Gilmour is handed the mic to sing lead vocals for the first time in ten years. He sings well, a song very much suited to his style, with a bitter-sweet tone and a realisation that even though 'thoughts may linger', perhaps the good times have gone. It's another good song with some typical Saga moments, most notably military-style rudiments from Negus to accompany the opening basslines and tight stab sequences to pave the way for Gilmour's vocal entrance. It's a shuffle, a rare Saga rhythmic approach, but it's effective, particularly with the striking guitar motifs, a great climbing guitar solo, fluent cymbal patterns, vigorous bass accents and excellent harmonies.

'Voila!' (1.42) (Saga)

This is a stunningly beautiful piece of art, featuring a 'solo' piano performance, with subtle keyboard accompaniment. For such a short track, there's a fair amount of texture and dynamics as Gilmour goes through his paces. The piece is technically dazzling and deeply expressive, his fingers moving effortlessly at speed whilst maintaining control and sensitivity. Malcome Dome in *Prog* in October 2021 commented that 'Gilmour's impressive skills on the piano and synthesiser are showcased on this track'. The shortest track by far is of equal importance to the album.

'No Man's Land' (5.20) (Saga)
'Voila' serves as an aperitif to 'No Man's Land' with only a momentary space before this track comes cruising straight in with the first verse. It's an interesting song more for its storytelling than its musical content, although, as always, that's impressive. The lyrics centre around Sammy, a young boy in the house alone during a riot outside: 'he grabbed his daddy's gun' and 'One little boy forced to hide, became a man from what he saw that night'. My educated guess is that these are from the imagination of Jim Crichton, based on his previous approach to storytelling in the 'Chapters' and the darker elements of the *Generation 13* album. These words are equalled by the quality of the music at a relatively urgent tempo of 135 bpm. There is a change of melody at the bridge, in which the focus is on Sammy's frustrations and fears: 'No one gives a damn, living in No Man's Land'. The song has a majestic instrumental segment at 3.14, one of the best on the album; everyone excels, with intricate and powerful phrasing and an exquisite guitar solo that incorporates some brisk shredding and two-hand tapping. We are then returned to a repeat of the bridge before a rapid fade out and the conclusion that this is another impressive and enjoyable track.

'Without You' (6.10) (Saga)
A poignant and heartfelt closer that feels like a resolution to the emotional journey throughout the album. It opens gently with synth pads and a count of four on the drumsticks, with Negus thumping out a series of vigorous polyrhythms, jungle style, but this soon transitions into a solid backbeat for nearly a minute before it all suddenly drops away, leaving Sadler and Gilmour's neat synthesiser backing to showcase the first verse. Sadler cries out his own romantic thoughts and observations about the pain and longing of separation from someone deeply important and the strong desire to reconnect. The second verse brings a more lively feel; the bass in particular is marvellous, with measured precision. The breaks between verse and chorus, although short, pack a lot in, including precise, melodious guitar hooks and nifty snare-to-tom drum fills. Three-quarters of the way into the song, the jungle beats return, with a few more background embellishments, heralding the eagerly anticipated guitar lead. You know it's coming and at 4.41, it's another sublime exhibition of skill and technique, including short, sharp, fast shredding (again) and sustaining of the highest notes – magnificent. As the jungle drums gradually retreat, the sounds from the opening track 'Entracte' reappear to close a majestic album. Welcome back, Saga.

Extra Track
'The Security Of Illusion (Acoustic Version)' (4.42)
Incredibly similar to the studio version, Sadler is in a more playful mode and Crichton's acoustic guitar rhythm and soloing are faultless. It's great to hear the song at its rawest.

Steel Umbrellas (1994)

Personnel:
Michael Sadler: vocals
Jim Crichton: bass
Jim Gilmour: keyboard, vocals
Ian Crichton: guitars
Steve Negus: drums, percussion
Paula Mattioli, Fred White, Stu 'The Rooster' Saddoris: backing vocals
Recorded and mixed at Goodnight L.A.B. Van Nuys, California
Produced by Jim Crichton and Saga
Recording engineer: Jim Crichton
Recording engineer (keyboards): Steve Negus
Mixed by Mike Ging
Digital mastering by Eddy Schreyer
Art direction and design: Vivid Images
Front cover concept and photography: Penny Crichton
Steel Umbrellas: Heidi Coyle
Running time: 40:34
Release date: 2 May 1994
Label: Polydor Records
Highest chart places: DE: 65, CN: did not chart, US: did not chart, UK: did not chart

Whilst on tour promoting *The Security Of Illusion,* American TV producer Stephen J Cannell enquired if the band would be interested in composing the soundtrack for his new TV show, *Cobra*. The songs had to be shorter, lighter and more commercial, thus *Steel Umbrellas* was created, causing confusion and concern amongst Saga fans. It was a risky but appealing idea, with the prospect of reaching a wider audience. Cannell had an excellent reputation as a TV producer and writer of cult series such as *The Rockford Files* and *The A Team*. *Cobra* wasn't anywhere near this calibre and bombed.

Gilmour:

> Had the TV series been a hit, then no doubt the album would have been, too, but the show was so bad that the CD died along with it. Even so, there are some great moments, such as 'I Walk With You' and 'Say Goodbye To Hollywood'.

Ian Crichton remembers the six months away from home and the laborious process of recording. Brother Jim agrees: 'The album should have had liner notes stating that this isn't really a Saga album, it's a TV series soundtrack.'

The opportunity could have been the greatest thing that they ever did, but the show was a flop and they made no money, or perhaps more importantly, it didn't enhance their reputation. They felt that because the album was so different than the rest, they thought of the name *Steel Umbrellas*, to protect them from backlash they anticipated from their fans.

Rich Wilson from *Prog* in October 2014: 'In hindsight, this was an ill-judged attempt to cross the mainstream. It failed to heighten the band's popularity and, understandably, caused a fleeting fan backlash against the slick, 1980s pop sound.' I'd say any Saga album is better than no Saga album and in truth, this isn't bad at all. The bonus on the SPV 2002 CD, remastered by Steve Negus, is 'I Walk With You (Live)', which also appears on the earMusic 2021 reissue.

'Why Not?' (4.17) (Saga)

Saga have never suffered from poor production and whatever is said about this record, you couldn't devalue the overall sound. This excellent choice of opener, following on from the previous album, only 15 months earlier, has all the hallmarks of Saga: solid guitar riffing, delightful synthesiser padding set to a meter at 122 bpm for most of the track. Lyrically, it's not that easy to interpret, presumably based on Saga's decision to take up the opportunity of writing the *Cobra* TV soundtrack, something they'd not done previously. Bang on two minutes is the album's first guitar solo, a short and sweet affair, possibly with airplay in mind. Likewise, the anticipated instrumental break and bridge, featuring the spoken word with megaphone-like effects, work well for a radio audience, which, of course, would also promote the TV series. The rest of the song is similar to the opening half, ending more thoughtfully than just a fade-out. This was deemed strong enough to be released as a single with 'Steamroller' on the flip.

'(You Where) Never Alone' (4.27) (Saga & Gerald O'Brien)

This track returns to a more sorrowful tone as befits the subject matter, a psychologically intriguing theme dealing with encouragement and reassurance, a similar theme to 'As I Am' from *Beginners Guide*: 'I'm coming out of the shadows to chase the demons from your door', stressing that help is always at hand. Writing credits on the original release are also given to Gerald O'Brien, a Canadian-born singer-songwriter and composer. Most prominent are the pulsating syncopated drum and bass rhythms driving the track, complemented by tastefully placed tom and rim shots, which feature during the quieter moments, as well as a crisp, attacking snare that resonates during the atmospheric effects injected through the guitar solo, perfectly suited to the song's aura. Multiple tracked and layered vocals also showcase the superior production, with sparse but effective use of reverb and delay. Chosen as another single from the album, this was coupled with 'Walking On Thin Ice'.

'Bet On This' (3.53) (Saga)

An innovative acoustic guitar intro, with a barely audible bell echoing in the distance, gives way to the main melody, which is presented as an instrumental initially before the first verse arrives. This track does feel more like a soundtrack than the others, because of its gradual build and understated arrangement, creating atmosphere without being overpowering, addressing the album's title with the first and only reference to 'Steel Umbrellas'. It's an introspective and pessimistic view on life, where the narrator bemoans the fact that things 'aint going so well' and if it's going to happen, hence the need to buy more insurance, 'It'll happen to me'. It's a well-constructed song, with notable aspects being the splendidly inventive and extremely classy lead guitar, energetic keyboard stabs and an appealing acapella ending.

'Shake That Tree' (4.17) (Saga)
The eerie, hypnotic keyboard pads that introduce the track, based on previous songs, lead you to believe that this is a Jim Gilmour song and you'd be right. It's a mid-tempo, relaxed, easy listening offering and very much suited to Gilmour's warm and high voice. The metaphor of 'shaking the tree' symbolises confronting complacency and taking responsibility for change. The words are the main feature in the track and are abstract, evoking a playful and upbeat feel rather than telling a clear story. Paula Mattioli (Cell Mates, Gypsy Queen) adds a pleasing velvety vocal in a call and response with Gilmore, harmonising in both verses and choruses, 'you go your way, I'll go my way'. Musically, there isn't too much happening during the instrumental section, but it does lead into a tasteful guitar solo. It's a pleasing track, with a strong chorus and some great mellow bass work.

'Password Pirate – Access Code – Password Pirate' (3.35) (Saga)
The temperature is lifted somewhat with this playful, upbeat, quirky number that sounds like nothing else on the album. The melody and groove are anchored fantastically by Crichton's bass runs that are smooth, infectious and exciting, reminiscent of Golden Earring's 'Radar Love'. Negus maintains a more solid beat and tight accenting throughout, as Sadler sings in a completely different style than we've heard previously. It's sharp, theatrical and rhythmically aggressive, almost rapping some of the lines and he does it extremely well. The theme seems to be a commentary on the emergence of the digital age and, in particular, issues with security: 'I'm a fat cat inside your Mac, I'll turn your mouse into a rat', says the narrator, gleefully advising, 'I'm inside of your machine'. It's a song that you can't really nod your head to, but you can revel in the almost improvised but instantly recognisable guitar parts of Ian Crichton. You get the impression the band enjoyed recording this and it would be a great live track if given the chance.

'I Walk With You' (4.02) (Saga)
A ballad sandwiched between two more upbeat tracks in which acoustic guitars and soft piano dominate the arrangement, with occasional string swells adding additional depth. There's a restrained drum pattern supporting the melody and the words, which tell of the loss of a loved one: 'It's days like

these that resurrect all the memories' and 'would you be proud or have I let you down?'. This does feel very much like a Sadler script and one that would potentially fit well into an episode of the *Cobra* TV programme this album was created for. As a standalone song, it's as good a ballad as Saga have done, being minimal instrumentally, leaving Sadler to own the emotion, something he is exceptionally good at. The beautiful acoustic guitar is an all too rare delight, providing an interlude between the vocals and a precursor to the long fade-out ending. Interestingly, it does appear on the *Detours Live* album, the only track on *Steel Umbrellas* that does make it to a live recording.

'Push It' (3.01) (Saga)
The dynamics increase with this short and sharp aggressive track at just over the three-minute mark, but it's packed with goodies, such as the bouncing basslines, playful vocals and subtle supporting synth patterns. It starts at a relentless pace featuring lively drum syncopation and heavy riffing before the solid backbeat signals the singing to begin. The opening two lines reflect the spirit and pace of pressing on in life and not looking back: 'I'm an adrenaline junkie, just can't get enough'. This is very much a lead vocal track with no overplaying or histrionics, with an effectively panned a cappella ending. It's an enjoyable track that I'd categorise as the younger brother of 'Password Pirate', particularly from a rhythmic perspective, as both are driven by a powerful and engaging drum beat.

'Steamroller' (4.12) (Saga)
The only song on the album with a one-word title and reading through the lyrics, it could well be about a steamroller. Perhaps one of the TV series episodes was to feature such a vehicle, or, more likely, it's just a collection of innuendos: 'so rub my bumper, nice and clean, if it's good for you, it sounds good to me'. The track is littered with them. Surely not, not Saga. Ian Crichton begins the track with a short, quirky guitar motif joined by a casual rhythm backing, a sequence of overlapping bass drum punches and a glorious funky bass guitar. Sadler's vocal style is smooth and cool with a laidback swagger, opening with 'You got my motor running, slide me into gear'. The chorus maintains the same attitude and flow with multiple repeats of 'Steamroller', followed by a range of 'comments' from what it would appear to be the vehicle itself, or is that just a metaphor, too? 'I'm built for comfort not for speed' and 'Oh, I've got everything that you need'. Summarising the track, there's nothing too spectacular or memorable apart from the earworm repetition of 'Steamroller', but the humorous lyrical content is different from Saga's usual themes, so it's an interesting approach.

'Say Goodbye To Hollywood' (4.33) (Saga)
Similar to 'Shake That Tree', Gilmour had to fly back to LA from Hollywood to finish the lyrics and the vocals. This is his second time singing lead on this

Above: When Jim Gilmour (top right) joined on keyboards for their third album, Saga's classic line-up was finally in place. (*Alamy*)

Left: Rene Zamic's illustration is as striking as the music on *Saga,* the 1978 debut, introducing a unique brand of synth-heavy prog. (*Maze Records*)

Right: *Images At Twilight* is the supreme second album. Tony Robert's artwork reimagined the alien 'Chapter' concept. (*Polydor*)

Left: Tony Roberts' illustration of *Silent Knight* is based on the Einstein Tower in Potsdam. Musically, it houses several Saga classics. (*Polydor*)

Right: Saga's most successful album, *Worlds Apart* was recorded in England with Rupert Hine, who transformed the band's sound. (*Maze Records/ Polydor*)

Left: The UK version of *Worlds Apart* was issued with a different sleeve. (*Portrait*)

Right: *Heads Or Tails* didn't reach the same heights as *Worlds Apart,* despite the strength of the songwriting and the expensive stage show. (*Maze Records/Portrait*)

Above: An early PR shot of Saga. Peter Rochon is second left, and Michael Sadler's moustache is centre. (*Edwin Ammerlaan*)

Below: A publicity shot from 1983 of a very young-looking Saga. (*David Gahr*)

Above: Michael Sadler and Steve Negus, who switched to the Simmons, a kit he helped to design. (*Edwin Ammerlaan*)

Right: A programme purchased at Hammersmith Odeon on 10 November 1983, containing some marvellous photographs and a detailed history up to that point. (*Authors Collection*)

Left: Three studios were used to record *Behaviour*, but the experience resulted in Negus and Gilmour leaving the band. (*Maze Records/Portrait*)

Right: *Wildest Dreams* saw Saga as a three-piece with Keith Olsen handling production. It has many fine songs, but it is very different from past records. (*Atlantic*)

Left: Still a trio, *The Beginners Guide To Throwing Shapes* is lively, musically challenging and thoroughly enjoyable. (*Penny Crichton*)

Right: The classic lineup return for *The Security Of Illusion,* which boasts great songs, immaculate production and Walter Gabrielson's brilliant painting (*Avalanche Records*)

Left: *Steel Umbrellas* sees Saga unsuccessfully attempting to reach a wider audience by recording a soundtrack for the TV series *Cobra*. (*Polydor*)

Right: Saga's concept album, *Generation 13*, is a monstrous 25-track story using clever orchestral arrangements. The original CD and the 2021 reissue cover are shown. (*Bonaire*)

Above: The band live on stage, executing a thrash bang ending led by Mike Thorne, who joined the band in 2012. (*Penny Crichton*)

Below: The Crichton brothers and Michael Sadler in perfect alignment in 2011. (*Bert Treep*)

Above: Jim Gilmour and his impressive keyboard rig. You can never have enough. (*Penny Crichton*)

Below: Ian Crichton showcasing his phenomenal soloing technique on the 2005 *Trust* tour, with Christian Simpson on drums. (*Bert Treep*)

Left: Saga do 'grunge' with *Pleasure And The Pain*, a dirty, gritty, guitar-driven release. This original cover is by Penny Crichton (*Bonaire*)

Right: Saga returned to their roots with a modern version of the first three albums on *Full Circle,* which reintroduced the 'Chapters' and Fabian Kraus's alien. (*SPV*)

Left: More high-quality artwork for *House Of Cards*, by Eric Fulghum. The 'Chapters' continue with impressive songwriting and performances. (*SPV*)

Right: The 'Chapters' end here, and it's Steve Negus' last Saga record. He ends on a high note with *Marathon*. (*SPV*)

Left: *Phase One* is a 'random' release with tracks that didn't make *Images At Twilight* and demos of the ones that did. (*SPV*)

Right: With a broadcast-themed concept, the cover of *Network* depicts previous albums, but it has a new sound and direction. (*SPV*)

Above: Jim Crichton is in the spotlight during the 2015 *Sagacity* tour. (*Alexander Mertsch*)

Below: Jim Gilmour during the 2017 *40*[th] *Anniversary And The Final Chapter* tour. (*Bert Treep*)

Above: See them smile. Michael Sadler and Dusty Chesterfield enjoy a moment on the 2022 *A Night To Remember* tour (*Bert Treep*)

Below: Jim Gilmour sings while the rest of the band wait for their cue during the 2022 tour. (*Bert Treep*)

Left: *Trust* was enthusiastically recorded and contains some of Saga's finest songs. It also boasts impressive artwork by Balazs Papay. (*InsideOut*)

Right: Michael Sadler bowed out temporarily after *10,000 Days*, which has all the trademark Saga elements and Warren Flanagan's inspired space-themed cover. (*InsideOut*)

Left: *The Human Condition* is Saga's only studio album not to feature Michael Sadler. Rob Moratti does a magnificent job writing and singing. (*InsideOut*)

Right: Sadler was back and on fine form with a well-constructed set of songs and exceptional instrumental passages on *20/20*. (*earMusic*)

Left: The last album of new material, *Sagacity* is a successful blend of experimentation and traditional Saga fare. (*earMusic*)

Right: Reimagined and reworked acoustic versions from the back catalogue. *Symmetry* is magnificent, and a must-have addition to the collection. (*earMusic*)

Left: An advert placed in *Kerrang!* in 1983 that lists the stores to buy *Worlds Apart* with the free limited edition lapel badge. (*Authors Collection*)

Right: A 1983 edition of *Kerrang!* advertising *Heads Or Tails*. The album reached number three on the import chart. (*Authors Collection*)

album and it's much quieter and more relaxed than track four. The title has been used by other artists, too, including Ronnie Spector (1977), Billy Joel (1981) and Eminem (2002). Saga's version tells the tale of an ageing movie star pining for the good old days. The lyrics are dripping with nostalgia, 'You were a star, you know you had it all', moving to, 'The future claimed you and you were left behind, the road you travelled has broken down with time'. The musical arrangement matches the lyrical sentiment, beginning with a soft, dulcet keyboard prelude, a gentle heart-beating rhythm and immersive background keys to add to the ambience. There's also an acoustic guitar in the background, the mix of acoustic and electric elements creating a rich tapestry of sound. The song is a bit mushy, but the band considered it a strong enough song to present a slightly revamped version on *Symmetry*.

'Feed The Fire' (4.09) (Saga)

The album wraps up with a slice of pure funk and you can understand why Saga fans didn't rate it as highly as the others. It's difficult to pinpoint where the influence and the musical direction came from for this track, as it is so different in style and feel from the rest of the album. Maybe it was the TV producers who insisted that the band move away from their more traditional rock-based writing and performance. However, it's still Saga, in experimental mode and to be fair, it isn't the most 'outrageous' piece of music they produced. The next two albums also veer away from what a Saga fan might expect. With this track being funk, the bass guitar plays a dominant role, brilliantly delivered by Crichton, demonstrating his versatility across different genres. Gilmour is also formidable, pumping out some absorbing rhythms, working with Negus in perfect unison. This strong pulse, with a steady sense of momentum, is easy to follow and therefore draws in the listener. Sadler is so laid back and casual that some words are barely audible, much of it being in a pseudo-rap style through some hefty effects. The potential was there to add some interesting enhancements, including more purposeful guitar and/or keyboard solos, but this doesn't quite materialise. The track is chorus-heavy and just fizzles out (pun intended), so ultimately it is disappointing, especially as the album's closer.

Generation 13 (1995)

Personnel:
Steve Negus: drums, percussion
Ian Crichton: guitars
Jim Gilmour: keyboards, vocals, clarinet
Jim Crichton: bass
Michael Sadler: lead vocals, pipe organ
Mary Newland: backing vocals on track 24
Richard Baker: orchestrations (with The Panorama City Philharmonic)
Recorded and mixed at The Goodnight Lab, Van Nuys, California
Produced by Jim Crichton
Additional production and engineering by Roger Sommers
Mixed by 'Hum, Buzz & Click' a.k.a. Roger Sommers, Shay Baby and Jim Crichton
Tracks 3, 7, 8, 15, 20 mixed by Mike Ging
Front cover concept: Penny Crichton
Art direction, poster concept: Ioannis for Vivid Images
Design, logo, typography: Stephen Jacaruso for Vivid Images
Photography: Heidi Coyle, digital paintings: Ioannis
Running time: 68:53
Release date: 26 June 1995
Label: Bonaire
Highest chart places: DE: 89, CN: did not chart, US: did not chart, UK: did not chart

Saga continued to tour across Europe, Canada and Puerto Rico. In addition, Jim Crichton worked on other projects in his studio, Sadler performed on sessions with Bobby Kimble for his 1994 *Rise Up* album, Ian released his solo album, *Welcome To The Boom Boom Room*, in 1995 and Gilmour worked on his solo album, *Instrumental Encounters*, released in 1996.

The inspiration for Saga's next venture was the book *13th Gen: Abort, Retry, Ignore, Fail*, written by Neil Howe and William Strauss and read by Jim Crichton. What resulted was a 25-song rock opera concept album exploring contemporary images of a dysfunctional family and the survival of the planet. In *Saga The Biography,* Jim Crichton explained:

> With *Steel Umbrellas*, we didn't make the kind of album we normally would make. We basically said to each other that there's zero chance that anything we do will get on the radio, so let's just make a completely nuts record. I wrote the script for it and hung it on the studio wall. We all sat down, wrote and recorded songs and treated it like a movie. It was 1995 and we were preparing to make a new album. Grunge was now the sound of the day, so we decided that it was a good time to make a concept album. *Tommy* and *The Wall* were both stories about children growing up and overcoming

problems, so we thought we'd be in good company if we followed that thread. Jeremy, the boy in our story, sets out on a journey to find his estranged father. The moral of the story is to be careful what you wish for.

Gilmore remembers it as a band effort, driven by Crichton, 'He would describe what sort of mood he wanted and I'd write something along the line musically. It was like a script we had to follow. It was a neat way to work and I'd like to do something like that again'. When the album was finished, Saga's European booking agent paid Crichton a visit and commented, 'Amazing album, but you guys are screwed. Record companies like records that fit into round holes or square holes; you've made an oval album.'

Jim Crichton came up with the idea of developing the album into a haunting story and invited the band to contribute to the music. Much of the material was created individually at the musicians' homes; the rest was a joint effort, composed together at Jim's Sound Image studio. This involved a large board in the studio detailing the sections of the story, so that the band wouldn't lose track of the parts they'd already covered. Ian Critchon managed to borrow and use on several of the tracks Greg Lake's semi-acoustic nylon guitar, as Emerson, Lake & Palmer were working nearby with Keith Olson at his Goodnight LA studio.

The album gradually and skilfully unfolds the science fiction-themed story of the young protagonist Jeremy, part of the so-called 13th Generation, who struggles with his identity and societal control and therefore sets out on a journey of discovery. He encounters Sam, a puppet and this has a major impact on him. The band adopt different characters within the 'play', which are detailed on the album sleeve.

This was Saga's most ambitious project so far, with over 70 minutes of captivating music that is best enjoyed in one sitting, with the lyrics to guide you through the creative chaos. Although not designed for radio play or to produce singles, it did reasonably well, making the charts in Germany. It would have made a fabulous stage show.

earMusic's 2021 reissue has a bonus of 'Gotta Love It' (1991 Single). The original CD version has a note dated 13 June 1995:

> Today, Sam seemed more miserable than ever. Over the past month, his whole personality has seemed to change. He is very angry and aggressive. But the good news is I've found my father and I think we will be meeting him on Monday. Jeremy.

'Chances Are #1' (1.42)

The first of the 25 tracks covering the concept. It's short, but definitely not sweet; rather, it immediately defines the dark and foreboding nature of the concept. It starts with a menacing, but exceptionally well-executed piano introduction from Gilmour. Sadler is on form, too, with a talking and singing combination that's downbeat and moody, delivering some cleverly constructed lines mournfully. A very short verse continues in the same vein, the vocal delivery continuing a sense of impending doom. At 1.20, piano and vocals disappear, leaving a synthesiser swelling and background noises preparing for the next instalment.

'Generation 13 (Theme #1)' (2.42)

This is an instrumental, but it does have Sadler in one of his many characters shouting out instructions in the background in what appears to be a train station: 'keep his hands away from the doors'. It's done so well that you can almost visualise the chaos of the scene. Ian Crichton is riffing and Negus unleashes a solid four on the floor beat as the volume and tension build. There's a quick increase in tempo with double bass drumming and a more urgent riff sequence for 15 bars, leading to another passage in which the keyboards dominate a cinematic landscape. This now feels like a soundtrack, as the orchestra is introduced briefly before the track's climax. This is new and exciting. Another 23 tracks and 64 minutes to go.

'All Will Change (Goodbye And Good Luck)' (1.57)

The piano introduction to this track forms one of the main motifs that runs throughout the album. Sadler delivers the vocal in a similar mode to track one, understated and fairly quiet, at times inaudible: 'I want to touch you, but if I touch you all will change'. The second passage is led by a legato piano with additional eerie words: 'I've been here watching you all through the night, why does it scare me so to look into your eyes'. There's a return to the opening passage, with a repeated 'All will change' before this piece ends, setting up the next instalment.

'The Cross (Home #3)' (4.06)

A spiritually tinged track and the most recognisable on the album because of its hook and powerful performance. It's also the only song on *Generation 13* that appears on any live release, three in total and could stand out on its own without necessarily being part of this concept. It evolves the story and introduces the main character, Jeremy, played by Sadler. Jeremy seeks guidance and understanding, something he symbolises in the form of a cross. Four bars of warm keyboard pads begin the song before the lead vocalist, Gilmour, in his soft, dulcet tones, narrates: 'the boy is here, he won't say much, I don't know why, one thing is clear, we know he's had a troubled life'. Jeremy responds: 'You are not who I had in mind, I don't know where I belong, but I'm sure it's not here'. The story unfolds with alternating performances from Gilmour and Sadler in their respective roles.

Instrumentally, Jim Crichton's melodic bass runs dictate the groove, with Negus locking in tightly and Ian Crichton's pinpoint phrasing adding some extra flavour. The chorus is energetic and passionate as Jeremy pleads forcefully, 'Father, when will I get my cross?' Negus skilfully solos underneath the vocals, creating even more tension. There are two more bars from the introductory section before the narrator delivers alternating lines with Jeremy. It's brilliant live, with Crichton switching from bass to Moog and Gilmour in full flight vocally and instrumentally.

'Danger Whistle' (0.45)
A spoken 'instrumental' consisting of inaudible background conversation and soundscapes, with a series of plucked strings from what sounds like a mandolin. The track is just an interlude to let the players get ready for the next scene.

'Leave Her Alone' (4.33)
More disturbing soundscapes and a lamenting organ open the track with 'victim' Jeremy cautiously and quietly narrating what he can hear, 'sometimes in the hall' and 'sometimes through the night'. There are three short verses and two minutes pass before Jim Crichton's intriguing bassline imitates footsteps. The soundscapes and voices increase and Negus executes three strokes on the toms, effectively utilising the space and then applying distant rudimentary snare accompaniment before the beat picks up and it's the rhythm section in full flight. It's a glorious passage and although there's plenty of instrumentation and voices in the background, you have to listen carefully to notice, as the main attention is on the rhythm section. The track concludes with a dead stop ending and a threat that sounds like 'Leave her alone'.

'I'll Never Be Like You #1' (0.43)
The opening aura of the previous track continues throughout this very short passage, but this time with a solemn 'church' organ and Jeremy is much sadder: 'I'm not sure what the future holds for me and I don't know where I'll go and who I'll meet, but I'll never be like you'. A reference to his father.

'My Name Is Sam (Finding A Friend)' (0:35)
There's no break from the previous track and it's straight into the introduction of a new character: 'My name is Sam'. Sam is played by either Jim Crichton or Roger Sommers, 'depending on if it's a good day, bad day, or he's just being sarcastic', as the liner notes say. It's still very atmospheric, but the main theme is a jerky affair made up of synth and guitar. It's mainly Sam and his disconcerting voice, deliberately and effectively low down in the mix: 'I hate this place, I'm swimmin' in the garbage', 'I need a hand'.

'The 13th Generation' (4.21)
This centrepiece of the album has a more technical and complex arrangement and a narrative that starts to better explain the scenario of humans being

engineered and controlled and the 13th Generation becoming self-aware: 'The year is 1945 and number 12 has now arrived, this is where we all came from, can you undo what we have done?' and in the next verse, 'it's time to face our own worst fears, the 13th generation is here and what you see is what you get, so take a seat we're not done yet'. A brief but tasteful guitar phrase begins, followed by solid bass drum and ambient keyboard pads, with multi-tracked vocals for the first verse, Sadler emphasising and harmonising the last word on each line. The second verse settles down to a more solid groove, then reverts back to the previous section for a change of narration and more effects-laden words from the character. The rest of the track is fundamentally a repeated sequence of the above and at just short of three minutes, Ian Crichton delivers an immersive 30-second guitar solo. 'The 13th generation's here!'

'The Cross #2' (2.02)
A reprise of an earlier theme from 'The Cross' with just Sadler in character and in conversation with his 'father', accompanied by gentle synthesisers and tasteful harmony vocals from Gilmore. It's another lyric-driven track with Jeremy becoming more inquisitive and still wanting to know, 'when will I get my cross'.

'The Learning Tree' (4.58)
The most ambitious and best track on the album in terms of musicianship. Everyone plays their part immaculately. It's a fantastic, powerful piece of music in 7/8 time with sufficient stops and starts to allow for more potent vocal delivery. Musically, it's a melodic, synth-driven progressive rock piece, blending atmospheric keyboards, powerful driving rhythms and reflective vocals. The climate is dictated by a warm bass with ongoing flourishes from synth and guitar, both panned for extra effect and classy fills from Negus. The lyric sheet within the sleeve is substantial, continuing the conversation between Jeremy and his father, it would appear, highlighting a long list of contradictions all contributing to Jeremy's state of mind. These include 'you gave me faith, you made me doubt myself' and 'you gave me truth, you made me disbelief'. Sam makes a brief appearance as one of the characters having conversations in the distance and across both speakers. It's a brilliantly constructed song and you almost forget this is part of the concept. It's another track that stands tall on its own.

'I'll Never Be Like You #2 (Once Again)' (3.59)
The tone is downbeat and depressing, in keeping with where we are in the story: Jeremy's realisation that he will never be like his father. Sadler expertly portrays his deeply sorrowful character: 'so once again I'm gonna have to make some changes, I might get lost along the way'. The orchestra plays a pivotal role in the soundscape, swelling and falling, the string

section being particularly emotive. A tremendous performance from Sadler and an inspired orchestral arrangement make the four minutes pass by quickly.

'Snake Oil' (1:07)
By complete contrast, this track has a weird and troubling circus theme – a dramatic switch from the last track. A steady build-up of a pipe organ takes you right back to being a child and sitting in the 'big top' waiting for the show to begin. The rhythm is odd and jerky with irregular, quiet cymbal splashes before the track morphs straight into the next one.

'We Hope You're Feeling Better #1 (The Test)' (4.57)
Starting with the organ that was building up during 'Snake Oil', it's now in full-blown circus mode with a recognisable motif and a series of accents prior to a 6/8 rhythm. It's all jolly, with the 'ringmaster' calling out, megaphone in hand, over the sound of the crowd: 'Good evening ladies and gentlemen'. It's pleasant until Sam appears in conversation again, unsettling and threatening, his voice higher up in the mix than others and panned to the right. The groove picks up at 1.05 before dropping to allow for more inaudible conversations. From 2.10, the rest of the track mainly consists of five identical repeats of the sing-along anthemic chorus, accented phrases as per the introduction and an excellent guitar lead. It's a splendid track that managed to find its way on *Symmetry* and the B-side of 'On The Loose', which also featured a remix of 'The Cross' and 'We Hope You're Feeling Better'.

'My Name Is Sam #2 (Your Time Is Up)' (2.34)
The track commences with an organ, a pulsing drum and bass heartbeat and repetitions of the 'cast' singing 'my name is Sam', the character himself intervening as the tale takes a more menacing turn: 'Your time is up, I'm the one who makes the decisions'. Most of the vocals are far down in the mix, good for effects and tension, but not necessarily to understand what's going on. The predominant lines, though, are clearly being uttered by Sam, who is starting to take control: 'I'm gonna roll your heart out and use it for a carpet'. The mood (thankfully) lifts a little at 1.16 with an interlude that's not previously been heard; it's upbeat and almost funky due to the punchy, syncopated bass and drum patterns and the smooth, vintage keyboard melodies, with their warm and nostalgic tones. The opening chaotic passage soon returns, with further repeats of 'My Name Is Sam', the final one being incredibly loud and distorted.

'Generation 13 (Theme #2)' (2.38)
This reprise is, in essence, an instrumental version of track two. It evokes the same sensation of being transported back to the train station with the

shouting echoing in the distance. This time, the main synthesiser is pulsating, eventually slowing down, grinding to a halt, exhausted. A swift drum fill brings in the hook, driven by a double bass drum pattern, leading into a brief, more standard beat with a crunchy guitar riff and a dead stop.

'Where Are You Now?' (1.20)

In three short verses with minimal synth backing over Ian Crichton's sublime acoustic guitar, Sadler resumes the story. It appears that Jeremy has now taken control, but what has he done? 'Oh where are you now, when I need you the most, I took your life as you lit up my smoke'. It's expressed in a miserable, depressing vein (great acting).

'Screw 'Em' (4.14)

The roller coaster of emotions and dynamics hurtles along as 'Screw Em' steams in with no gap from the previous track. It's an instantly likeable song, not least because of Negus' breakbeats and Ian Crichton's main signature guitar melody for a 35-second opener. There are some smart instrumental bridges across the song and the vocals are slightly more pronounced, sung with an air of defiance as the story unfolds, 'take a good look, what do ya see? Do you really think you're so different from me?' The second verse is particularly poignant as it consists of four 'rules' or pieces of advice that are 'simple as hell'. Gain confidence, make them sign the cheque, look out for number one, take the money and run.

What follows this is one of the best passages on the album. In one minute and 13 seconds of astounding lead guitar, Ian Crichton displays how inventive and dexterous he really is in breadth and depth, with some stunning runs both intricate and intense. Not to be overlooked, though, are Negus and the Jim Crichton, who are tight and solid with some dynamic accenting and driving grooves. There's a brief reminder of the story with a short refrain of 'we'll never be like you' before returning to the opening section for a good minute or so. The outro is relatively long, but the riff and rhythms are strong enough to warrant this.

'No Strings Attached' (5.20)

The ending of 'Screw Em' feeds straight into this track, which takes us on another contrasting musical journey. The feel is smooth and mellow with more subtle guitars and keyboards and a 6/8 meter, allowing more breathing space with less emphasis on the backbeat. The breaks remind me very much of Steely Dan and their use of Hawaiian-style guitar sounds. It's clean, lightly compressed with chorus and subtle reverb and played with smooth slide phrasing and sustained vibrato to create a fluid, steel-like tone. The chorus, 'No strings attached', is delivered acapella, with Gilmour's voice being the most prominent and it's highly effective. There are extended instrumental segments, but the feel and tempo don't change throughout the song. Lyrically, it's a series of questions from Sam, all starting with 'Do you think it's time', with the menacing connotations still there, 'that I sharpened the blade', 'I tried to touch you'.

'All Will Change #2 (It's Happening To Me)' (2.00)
Another reprise, this time from track three, with a similar format consisting of Gilmour's exquisite piano and Sadler's despondent vocal delivery, the most disturbing being the last two lines of the four, 'I look in the mirror I don't like what I see, what you've become, is happening to me'. The track gradually fades out, adding to the haunting effect.

'The Victim' (2.59)
The church organ returns, loud and proud, to reconnect the story and as a prelude to another slice of 'Saga by numbers' guitar and synth interactions and solid rhythms – it's magnificent. We're treated to guitar flourishes after each vocal line, with complementary solo bursts and Sadler singing more like himself, although he is still in character, as Gilmour adds more deft synthesiser melodies.

It's a short but excellent track and, as much as any of the others, you can fully appreciate the quality of the clean and bright production as every instrument has immaculate clarity and presence.

'One Small Step' (3.25)
A track described as a 'Spoken Instrumental', delivered by Sam, it's eerie and creepy and best experienced with headphones on in a darkened room to get the full impact. The backdrop is keyboards blended with an orchestra. This is big, cinematic stuff and it's colossal. The orchestra is magnificent in controlling the mood swings. Stirring stuff.

'Sam's New Friend' (2.30)
Noted as another 'spoken instrumental', but it's not really. A cinematic opening begins proceedings; it's as though you're still sitting in the movie theatre listening to Sadler in operatic mode: 'Where are you now, when I need you the most' and even a cry of 'when will I get my cross'. The orchestral production is monumental and the track cleverly incorporates elements of previous themes, in particular 'The Cross', where the band also add additional touches and embellishments, such as drum fills, to differentiate from what's gone before.

'We Hope You're Feeling Better #2' (1.21)
The track segways from the previous song and is a reprise of track 14. It's very similar but more orchestral and the previous circus feel has been added to ensure continuity with the story, which is now coming to an end. The melody is identical to the previous version, with just the two choruses sung.

Mary Newland is credited with singing the backing vocals and does add a more harmonious texture.

'Chances Are #2' (1.36)

The concluding song of the whole saga and a return to track one to wrap things up. Musically, it's the same sublime piano melody, but lyrically, there are some changes in the first verse: 'Imagine if you will having more than you had planned and now that it's all yours you just can't wait to wash your hands'. The second verse is a repeat of the first four lines from the opening track and the final words are 'Chances are, it just might come true' before the track, the album and the tale vanish.

Bonus Track On The 2021 Reissue

'Gotta Love it' (1991 Single) (4.41)

A powerful drum introduction and guitar riff give the impression that the track is going to be heavier than it is, but it soon settles into a pop song typical of the late 1980s and early 1990s, with bright synthesisers, gated-reverb drums, polished production and catchy, hook-driven melodies designed for radio. The chorus is catchy and Sadler does well to hit the highest notes; there's a guitar solo and a sing-along, clap-along section. Great performances, immaculate production and very radio-friendly.

The Saga Softworks (1995)

Produced and created by Brian Foraker, Dave Benson and Todd Herman. This is a CD-ROM described as 'An Interactive Anthology'. The back of the CD crystal case explains that this multimedia CD-ROM features 179 song samples, two previously unreleased full-length videos and 'worldwide website simulation'. It was truly groundbreaking. The CD audio features eight audio tracks from *Generation 13*, including an edited version of 'The Learning Tree' not available anywhere else. There is a fairly in-depth explanation of 'System Requirements' for 'Windows' and 'Macintosh', but it's unlikely to play on more modern systems.

Pleasure And The Pain (1997)

Personnel:
Michael Sadler: vocals
Ian Crichton: guitars
Jim Gilmour: keyboards, vocals
Glen Sobel: drums
Jim Crichton: bass
Additional vocals: John Bianchini, Thomas Korg
Recorded and mixed at Sound Image Entertainment Studios, Van Nuys, California, except 'Pleasure And The Pain', recorded and mixed at Empire Studio by John Bianchini
Produced by Jim Crichton, except tracks 4 and 8 by Jim Crichton and Stretch
Engineered by John Henning and Stretch (Raul Mora)
Art direction and design by Ioannis and Steven Jacaruso at Vivid Images Interactive
Band photography by Penny Crichton
Front cover model on Bonaire release: Joelle Spoonhour
Running time: 44.18
Release date: 7 April 1997
Label: Bonaire
Highest chart places: DE: 93, CN: did not chart, US: did not chart, UK: did not chart

How on earth do you follow an album like *Generation 13*? Saga had a go with 1997's *Pleasure And The Pain*, which sees them journeying into grungier territory. It also contains some unusual choices, including a cover of The Beatles 'Taxman' and a revitalised version of 'You're Not Alone'. Steve Negus wasn't available due to a busy personal schedule and was replaced by Glen Sobel in the studio and Graham Lear on stage for the subsequent tour.

Gilmour recalled that the album was written and recorded in five weeks and could understand why it shocked a lot of fans, 'it shocked me, too'. He didn't particularly like the writing or recording and I can understand that, as there wasn't the same opportunity for keyboards, but he did agree that at the time it was the closest they could get to sounding contemporary. 'We tried to reinvent the band', said Jim Crichton. 'There's some good stuff on it, done pretty quickly and there aren't many keyboards – it is very raw.' The lack of keys enabled brother Ian to step up and out of all the band members, he likes it the most, but 'not all of it'. In the 2016 CD reissue liner notes, Sadler admitted that, for a while, they weren't quite sure of what the fans wanted to hear, but they had to stay competitive:

> On one hand, we had switched to a kind of survival mode, looking for a contemporary Saga sound so that we could continue to be part of the rock music scene. On the other hand, we wanted to stick to our typical

trademarks and stay true to our own style. It was the time of trial and error in which we composed material for this album, which is apparent in the album's rawer sound.

The cover was originally a girl's tongue being pierced with a thick rod, but the record company in Germany thought it was sadistic, so they came up with the 'Garbage Can' concept. Perhaps a shrewd marketing campaign, as Saga fans will probably have both versions. I much prefer Penny Crichton's original design. Check out her website for more details.

The album was released on the eve of Saga's 20th anniversary tour, 13 June being exactly 20 years since their very first performance. Offenbach was selected as the venue and they were joined by special guest John Wetton. He and Saga performed 'Only Time Will Tell' from Asia's self-titled album. The concert was filmed and was available on VHS to be sold at subsequent shows. During this period, Saga were presented as 'Cultural Ambassadors' by the Canadian Prime Minister.

Bonus tracks on the reissues are: 'Welcome To The Zoo' (Live), 'Time To Go' and 'You're Not Alone' (both from 2016's *Live In Hamburg*) and 'Solsbury Hill' (1991 Single).

'Heaven Can Wait' (6.13) (Saga)

A gradual ascension of a guitar and keyboard gently eases in the song, with a confident and controlled Sadler singing the first two verses, the second verse including added instrumentation and vocal harmonies to lift it slightly. The chorus is much heavier, showcasing the new production style and it really is in stark contrast to any of Saga's other albums. It's gritty, grungy, raw, distorted and industrial and this continues throughout the whole album to a greater or lesser degree. Glen Sobel's sound is tight and punchy and during some of the verses, he introduces cross-sticking instead of the traditional snare back-beats to add more flavour. The guitar is well up in the mix, front and centre, less polished but with a more aggressive edge. This is a creative period for Ian Crichton, with his first solo album, *Ghettos By Design* – an incredibly progressive, heavy, raw and hard-hitting album – also released in 1997. The breaks allow for more subtlety, but the track is all about the catchy chorus, the standout guitars, some lightning-fast fills by Sobel and straight-ahead rock basslines keeping it all together. The track finishes like many Saga tunes, with a repeat of the opening phrases, keeping it fairly long at just over six minutes.

'How Do You Feel?' (4.05) (Saga)

The track opens with a distorted guitar accenting on the count of three and Sobel's very trashy offbeat hi hat accompaniment, as he attempts to tear through his snare skin. It's a song that's a combination of 3/4 and 4/4. Sobel's drumming approach is different from Negus and Cress; it's tight and articulate with a heavy edge, blended with crisp ghost notes and sharp accents. Vocal delivery speeds up during the chorus, squeezing the words in with more exasperation and urgency in contrast to the relaxed verses, which allow the vocals to cut through more. A series of tom rolls and a standard backbeat support the guitar solo during the bridge, then it's back to the chorus and a fade-out ending. It's a decent enough track with a loose feel and unusual chord progressions that sound fresh and quirky and don't follow the usual pattern you might expect from Saga – a combination of System of a Down and Rush, so certainly contemporary at the time.

'Welcome To The Zoo' (4.28) (Saga)
Another track favoured by Ian Crichton and you can see why. It's very guitar-heavy, with high-energy, dominant riffing over strong, pulsating rhythms and that very loud snare crack. The effects on Sadler's vocals reduce its volume in the mix a tad, but that doesn't make it any less menacing: 'Annie's got a thing about leather, Bobby's got a thing about lace'. The next two verses are just as obscure and the whole song seems to be a satirical look at society, likening modern life to a zoo where everyone is observed and controlled: Sadler cries out, 'Someone tell me what the hell is going on'. Synthesisers shine with simple but potent phrasing during the instrumental section as a precursor and backing for the guitar passage, which is similar to the previous track in style, sound and execution – gritty, heavy and distorted. There's effective use of feedback and other spontaneous noises to close and I'd conclude that this rough and crunchy track would be great live and fortunately, it does appear as such on the 2002 album reissue.

'Where's My Money?' (5.17) (Saga)
Where's my Money? Where's my Saga? What the hell is going on? This is about as far away from Saga as you can get. I'm all for experimental, but crikey. Ian Crichton admitted that he doesn't care too much for the track and I'll bet the vast majority of Saga fans don't either. However, in context, it makes sense as it is rebellious, defiant, even mutinous and it sums up the band's desire to do as they please. They've certainly done it with this track, which is labelled as an instrumental, with 'Where's My Money' bellowed throughout the track. Also yelled in the distance are 'Don't Be Late' and 'Wind Him Up', so again, a neat use of previous song titles. It's a dance/house track at 139 bpm, done with riotous aggression. It features weird synthesiser patterns, an almost relentless four on the floor driving rhythm, offbeat open hi hat accenting and a really heavy guitar riff for the main 'melody', which is a joy. There are a variety of sections, with the whole band 'improvising' to break up what is a lengthy five-plus minutes. It's all a bit messy, but perhaps so was the management of their finances, hence them wanting to know where the money's gone.

'You're Not Alone '97' (4.17) (Saga)
Perhaps in an attempt to forge an arch between the past and the present, some 18 years after it first featured on *Images At Twilight*, Saga reimagine 'You're Not Alone', adding '97' on the end to emphasise the difference. And they are not the same except for the iconic pre-chorus and chorus that are almost identical in words and melody. The '97' version has been written and styled to match the attitude and feel of *Pleasure And The Pain*. Jim Crichton wrote the original lyrics; he may have done so here, too, but it seems more likely to have been Sadler, particularly with the abrupt phrasing and more observational style, such as 'You lie for it, you die for it'. The number kicks off with a series of short double-strummed guitar riffs, soon joined by the rest of the band for the first verse. The middle eight is an extended instrumental section with cleverly introduced flavours of the original: the chanting of the track title and the main melody from the chorus, but with a greater reliance on guitar rather than keyboards. In the 2016 CD reissue liner notes, Sadler commented that he thought 'the '97' version is definitely worth hearing and an absolute success in its own way.' I can live with both, but it's the original version for me.

'Taxman' (3.35) (George Harrison)
An interesting choice of song and perhaps more to do with the title, harking back to 'Where is my money' than the music itself, but it does make a great cover track. It transpired that Sadler was singing the lyrics to 'Taxman' because he didn't have lyrics for a song they were working on at the time. Sadler in the 2016 CD reissue liner notes:

> I've always been a fan of The Beatles, so this kind of cover version was a natural consequence. We weren't all that keen on reinterpreting one of their obvious hits but preferred to work on one of their lesser-known songs. As tax, money and financial matters were on our minds in the 1990s, we felt 'Taxman' fit really well.

Arranged, performed and produced in keeping with the rest of this album, it's heavy, distorted and angry and all in all, it's a pretty good version. Crichton launches into it with dirty riffing, sparked by Sobel's opening assault, including the now customary syncopated bell of the ride patterns. It's superb drumming and bass playing, holding the melody together as McCartney and Starr did on the original. It stays true to much of The Beatles' version in its structure and I think Saga have done it justice.

'You Were Made For Me' (3.44) (Saga)
This isn't another cover version as per 'Freddie And The Dreamers' (Columbia 1963), but it does have a sense of an earlier version of Saga, with keys and guitar jointly opening up and Crichton's creeping lead runs being prominent

throughout. Sobel nails the shuffle and sixteenths to create the meter and it's Gilmour's turn for lead vocals, which are low in the mix. It's Jim, but not as we know him; he's immersed in effects when in both 'whispery' and 'shouty' mode. The song seems to be about exerting power and control over someone, exemplified by the macabre sentiment: 'I don't care if I live or die, just be there when I arrive'. The instrumental bridge is magnificent, fronted by a punchy guitar riff over keyboard pads and a stabbing rhythm section. It's a phenomenal segment and the best part of the album. I really like this track, but production-wise, the vocals could have been handled better.

'Gonna Give It To Ya' (3.56) (Saga and Stretch)
A smoother timbre than before and a more positive mood, with the bass's energy and fluidity pushing the groove, right across the track, with several very impressive runs from Jim Crichton. This is more defined and obvious due to a lack of snare backbeat; instead, just a constant bass part keeps time, just like Bowie's 'Panic In Detroit'. Sobel is still there, though, with a series of timely fills. It's a solid enough track with two verses, several choruses, a bridge and enough variations of the main theme to keep it interesting with super lead breaks from both Gilmour and Ian Crichton.

'Fantastically Wrong' (5.47) (Saga)
A track that's very short on words – 47 in all, of which 17 are repeated – this is more about the musical attitude than it is about the lyrical meaning. Some of these include 'paranoid', 'schizoid', 'freakazoid', 'sci-fied', 'French fried' and they sneak in 'don't be late', another previous song title. So it delves into darker territory, with its introspective lyrics and sense of realisation and disillusionment. This is inferred from note one with a chilling guitar intro, which is repeated during the track and the vocals are multi-tracked to emphasise the 'yelling' of the words mentioned above. The rest of the track is a blend of occasional quieter sections and more roaring guitar riffing and drum fireworks. Crichton and Sobel have been given licence to go berserk here, with some exceptional playing, but this track, as much as any of the others, suffers from a lack of clarity, so it's more difficult to identify what else is going on and that's a shame.

'Pleasure And The Pain' (2.35) (Saga)
The shortest track on the album is a fitting concluder, although it's completely different from the other nine tracks as the grunge filter has been lifted and perhaps thrown away forever! The first verse is sung solo by Sadler (very low in the mix) and is a direct lift from the classic crooner song 'My Way' by Frank Sinatra, with 'My Way' cleverly omitted from the last line. The rest of the words seem original and once again have references to previous tracks, 'Wildest Dreams' and 'No Stranger', the latter being important here as this track includes the first and final segment from 'No Stranger', played on a

delightful acoustic guitar by Ian Crichton and sung ably by Gilmour. The lyrics perhaps reflect on the highs and lows of existence and that pleasure cannot exist without pain. The final line may be highlighting the experience of creating this record or just the general experience of being in Saga: 'It's all been a pleasure, no pain'.

Bonus Tracks

'Welcome To The Zoo' (Live Version)

Included on the 2002 SPV reissue

Introduced by Sadler as being from the new album *Pleasure And The Pain*. A good quality recording, extremely well played and as near to the studio version as you'd want.

'Solsbury Hill' (Peter Gabriel) (1991 Single)

Included on the 2021 earMusic reissue

The challenge is how to approach such an iconic track, so the choice was to produce an almost identical replica. They did and it works. Great vocal delivery by Sadler with fabulous support from the rest of the band. It doesn't fit with the feel or production approach on *Pleasure And The Pain*, but it's a worthy addition to the Saga portfolio.

Full Circle (1999)

Personnel:
Michael Sadler: lead vocals and keyboards
Jim Gilmour: lead keyboards and vocals
Ian Crichton: lead guitar and acoustic
Steve Negus: drums and percussion
Jim Crichton: bass, keyboards and acoustic guitar
All songs written by Saga
Additional vocal recordings by Thommy Korge at The Bat Cave Bar and Grill Studio and John Bianchini at Empire Studios
Produced, recorded and mixed by Jim Crichton at Sound Image Studios, LA, California
Mixed by Brian Foraker
Front cover painting by Fabian Kraus
Cover design and graphics by Penny Crichton for Picture This Productions, Inc.
Running time: 48:21
Released date: September 1999
Label: SPV
Highest chart places: DE: 44, CN: did not chart, US: did not chart, UK: did not chart

Full Circle returned Saga to the tried and trusted formula that had been absent over the more recent releases. Back were the prominent keyboards and the opportunity to further enhance their songwriting and performing prowess. This was a welcome return and Saga fans voted with their wallets as concert tickets and album sales increased. The Saga tour between October and November 1999 and January 2000 saw ticket sales double compared to their previous tour.

Ian Crichton told Ammerlaan that 'Saga almost trapped themselves'. The previous albums had a different style, but with *Full Circle* and *House Of Cards*, they were back at the early Saga sound. 'I do like playing the new stuff a lot,' Gilmore added, 'it was agreed to just write what Saga would write.'

On sharing their collective input, they were all 'blown away' by the quality of the writing and the strength of the songs, amassing over 30 numbers before whittling them down. Part of the writing and arranging process included the philosophy that 'less is more' and it was about incorporating dynamics and instrumentation that could be replicated live. The 'Chapters' had also returned, pulling the Saga albums back together. In the 2021 reissue liner notes, Gilmour added:

> *Full Circle* is often referred to as Saga's return to form after a couple of experimental outings. The return of instrumental arrangements, duet lines from Ian and me and sold-out shows. There are some great vocal moments throughout the whole album. Quite a few of my keyboard performances were recorded into the sequencer on my Korg Trinity while on a ship.

Matthias Mineur's liner notes on the 2021 reissue explained, 'Continuing the conceptual and musical success of the first five albums, the term *Full Circle* refers to remembering your origins and returning to them'. Steve Negas agrees, commenting on the album on the 2003 *Silhouette* DVD:

> It definitely does feel like a full circle; we've come back to what we were in an earlier time. I think we realised that we'd missed out on some of the things that worked so well that were inherent in Saga music, like the earlier albums that people still love. I think we fleeted back to what we were doing to recapture some of that magic that happened in the first three albums.

Jim Critchton also noted that the close interaction of guitars, bass and keyboards reanimated their typical trademark. The songs on *Full Circle* have similarities to the initial trio of records, with the characteristic blend of haunting rock songs, quiet numbers and unusual tracks with interesting sounds.

'Remember When (Chapter 9)' (5.20) (Saga)

Up first is 'Chapter 9', following on from 'No Stranger (Chapter 8)', 18 years earlier, on *Worlds Apart*. Lyrically, there are references to previous song titles: 'Do you remember when I said don't be late' and 'It's time to turn another page'. This is my favourite track on the album, although it does have significant competition. It opens with a pulsating bass, a great tension builder and complementary synthesiser pads on the Korg Triton, playing a gentle verse melody to welcome in the vocals and the rest of the band. It's mid-tempo at 127 bpm and much more restrained and controlled than the previous album, perhaps even easing back on the throttle a little too much. It is a welcome return to a more keyboard-oriented flavouring, the dexterous Gilmour playing two synths at once when on stage. Structurally, it's fairly standard stuff, with four short verses, six choruses, a middle eight, catchy keyboard passages and an impressive guitar solo. The track is anchored by a fabulous, memorable guitar riff, great vocals and excellent arrangements. Although it doesn't really move the 'Chapter' concept on, it's a suitable opener, with Sadler asking, 'How are you, have I made you wait?' Yes.

'The One' (4.21) (Saga)

Ian Crichton opens with an iconic guitar riff. I suspect the way this is played live is not that dissimilar to how it was recorded in the studio, on a Marshall Micro Guitar combo, currently retailing at less than £30.00! On stage, Sadler holds his vocal mic in one hand and the mini speaker in the other whilst Ian Crichton riff's away. A brilliant teaser before the band stampede in to double the riff. This is a slightly slower pulse than the first track at 123 bpm, giving a more mellow and methodical feel, but the catchy riff and effective arrangement are just as appealing. The chorus drops to primarily vocals and keyboards, with Negus' archetypal 16ths on the hi hat and booming bass drum keeping time. The instrumental bridge features some restrained but still impressive lead guitar. Great performances all round, but it's the guitar riff and the staccato piano, a few notches down in the mix, that are most memorable. It's an excellent song, but I do wonder if this would have been more impactful with a slightly quicker tempo.

'Follow Me' (5.07) (Saga)

'Follow Me' has a more reflective and philosophical tone, as we glimpse into the narrator's thoughts, sometimes from a childhood perspective, but its theme is not obvious. In the verses, there are frequent repeats of 'where were you' by Gilmour, followed by a variety of lyrical responses from Sadler. The choruses are just Gilmour with minimal accompaniment: 'follow me, down the road, take my hand and don't let go, close your eyes and count to ten, round and round and back again'. The singing is wonderfully expressive whilst a charmingly strummed acoustic guitar plays alongside. It's this refrain that also starts the track, developing into a gentle 6/8 for the verses. The choruses are garnished with children's voices singing along gently, in some ways similar to Pink Floyd's 'Another Brick In The Wall (Part 2)' but without that intent and aggression. There are also tender moments during the break at 3.26, with a smooth synth solo, which does remind me of something that Styx would create, due to its rich analogue textures and melodic layers.

'Uncle Albert's Eyes (Chapter 13)' (5.22) (Saga)

Being 'Chapter 13', it's more difficult to piece together the story because 'Chapter 12' doesn't appear until *Marathon* four years later, but that's the point: to enjoy the puzzle and keep buying the albums. However, this track does give some clues and it focuses on Albert Einstein: 'See the man sitting in the corner feeling humble, can't you see the tears in Uncle Albert's eyes'. So, he's beginning to see more clearly what he needs to do. There's a great line or two also in verse three: 'You've read the news but we all forgot that the garden of Eden is a parking lot'. A clever satirical twist that an ideal world (Eden) has been replaced by something mundane and utilitarian (a parking lot). Keyboards begin playing the main verse melody and Sadler cautiously advises, 'get ready for a big surprise'. It's a slower, more purposeful groove in the chorus with vocals high in the mix, Sadler executing the high, sustained notes superbly as he sings the song's title. It's a fairly routine structure up to 2.34 until a brief repeated stab sequence launches the instrumental section, with fabulous twin leads courtesy of Gilmour and Ian Crichton and a short solo by the latter leading to the rest of the band dropping out for a synth to welcome in the fourth and final verse. A track with technical virtuosity aplenty and an atmospheric fading outro to prepare for 'Chapter 14', also on *Marathon*.

'Home' (5.06) (Saga)
A simple but assertive bass drum and cross-sticking pattern support a tastefully subtle Ian Crichton on acoustic guitar to initiate the track for almost a minute before the vocals appear. There's a similar feel to 'Follow Me', with Sadler in a sombre mood, except for the very short chorus – 'You can always go home, I think it's time to go home' – where he is more defiant, even annoyed. At 3.47, the song becomes a shade more energetic with a prominent keyboard pattern and sprightly tom rhythms before dropping down to the next verse. It's an acceptable vocal-based track with an elementary structure and some appealing instrumentation, mainly synth padding, with a theme centred around the desire for comfort and familiarity in an emotional or physical place where you'll be at peace, 'safe and warm'. It was strong enough to be a single, paired with 'The One'.

'Don't Say Goodbye' (5.33) (Saga)
One of Gilmour's favourite songs and another one where he and Sadler split the lead vocals to great effect. This definitely adds an interesting dimension, showcasing their different vocal styles and tones. Soft synths give the song a melancholy and reflective quality to this ballad, touching on the pain of separation and the fear of loss, perfectly suited to Sadler's capacity to express vulnerability during the verses, whilst Gilmour looks after the choruses: 'Don't say goodbye, 'cause you're already gone'. The dreamy, melodic keyboard sequence elevates the chorus. At 3.20, there's an outstanding instrumental section set up by a stepping bassline and a wonderful guitar solo, nothing too intricate, just well-constructed and rich in texture that's not overwhelmed by the rest of the band. It's a modest track, but extremely likeable and offers a good contrast to the rest of the songs. It doesn't appear on any of the live releases, more's the pity.

'Time Bomb' (4.05) (Saga)
Gilmour and Sadler share vocals again in a call-and-response that's fascinating to watch on stage (*All Areas – Live In Bonn 2002*). Lyrically, the song symbolises pressure, stress, or the inevitability of some impending event. The opening refrain picks up from the previous track with dominating booming bass and a mid-tempo groove with a snare thwack that's soaked in either reverb, echo, or both, designed to create anxiety. 'Where were you today?', asks Gilmour. Sadler repeats, 'I'm not sure if I should tell you' and thus it goes on for much of the song. Sadler chants the chorus, 'Can't you see I'm ticking like a time bomb, won't somebody come and light my fuse?' A great line supplemented by a superb quintessentially Ian Crichton guitar hook, which carries the song and is even more impactful in the final few seconds of the track. Gilmour raises the pitch during the vocal bridge and I note the word 'stranger' appears yet again. At 2.53, the much-anticipated lead guitar break is thoughtful and creative, but far too short. On the 2021 reissue liner

notes, Matthias Mineur describes this as a fan favourite and it is, but I feel there is just something lacking.

'Not This Way (Chapter 10)' (5.04) (Saga)
You just know from the gentle introduction that it's going to be a Gilmour song and it's a 'Chapter', usually written by Jim Crichton and sung by Sadler, but Gilmour handles it well and continues the story from 'Chapter 9', also on this album. He narrates, it would appear, from the alien's perspective: 'It seems like a thousand years, that I have watched you on your own' and 'and in the last fifty years you haven't had a lot to say' and from the closing chorus, 'You know I wanted to help you, but not this way'. The intro, like the whole song, is quiet, subdued, dark and ominous, with a beautiful acoustic guitar and an almost flute-like keyboard playing the main melody. It's a haunting and atmospheric scene, with Gilmour singing over an eerie backdrop of occasional bass notes, distant bells, acoustic soloing and synth pads. There's a brief return to the intro and the concluding lyrics to end, setting up 'Chapter 11' on the next album. It's not single material or an obvious choice to include in a live set, but it had to appear on *Chapters Live*.

'A Night To Remember' (5.44) (Saga)
This track is back to a more standard rock approach with a solid groove and impressive interplay between the guitar riff and keyboard arpeggios, both playing separate pieces but combining supremely. The song could have stood a quicker tempo, clocking in at 104 bpm for the majority of the track, making it a tad 'ploddy', but it still has a powerful riff and contains some admirable ingredients that are typical Saga, including expansive and orchestrally layered keyboards. Sadler and Gilmour are at it again, alternating lead vocals, with a range of sophisticated lyrics and precocious rhyming, such as 'position' with 'indecision', 'conversation' with 'concentration' and 'situation' with 'infatuation'. In a reflective observation of the subject, who is trying to make the most of life, Gilmour asks the question, 'Do you know what you're waiting for and how long it will take?' At this point, most of the instruments drop out to provide the light and shade. A tremendous guitar solo, that could have been lengthened, tight fills from Negus and a supreme vocal performance are the highlights of a likeable track, but it's perhaps just a bit too safe.

'Goodbye' (3.59) (Saga)
When *Full Circle* was released, there was a certain amount of speculation regarding the final track's message: would this be Saga's last album? It was their 13th and following a turbulent last few years, would they call it a day? Not so and why would they? We were still mid-'Chapter' and there was plenty to say musically and lyrically and as it turned out, there were nine more bundles of original material to release. 'Goodbye' was actually written about

Sadler's father, with whom he'd had a troubled relationship. The final verse is the most potent set of words, leading up to the line, 'and I will always remember, the day that we looked at each other and said … Goodbye'. Gilmour commented that it is 'one of the most emotional songs we've ever done, influenced by our Celtic roots', I suspect because of their strong sense of cultural identity and ancestral pride. The track borrows from similar passages within the album, such as the delicate, sustained synthesiser chords, expressive mellow guitar hooks, incorporating controlled feedback and a wide range of technical artistry from the band. From 1.41, the song is all about Sadler, expressive and passionate, longingly holding onto each note, especially the last one, displaying his incredible range. An emotional and fitting way to conclude a magnificent album.

House Of Cards (2001)

Personnel:
Ian Crichton: guitars, background vocals
Jim Gilmour: lead keyboards, vocals
Steve Negus: drums, percussion
Michael Sadler: lead vocals, keyboards
Jim Crichton: bass, keyboards
All songs written by Saga
Recorded at Sound Image Studios, Van Nuys, California
Produced and recorded by Jim Crichton
Mixed by Mike Ging at Sound Image Studios, Van Nuys, California
Front artwork by Eric Fulghum
Cover design and graphics by Penny Crichton for Picture This Image, Inc.
Running time 49:56
Released date: 12 February 2001
Label: SPV
Highest chart places: DE: 34, CN: did not chart, US: did not chart, UK: did not chart

The eagerly awaited follow-up to *Full Circle* took just 17 months to arrive in the record shops and not only were Saga fans anticipating an album just as good in every sense, but there was the matter of additional pieces of the 'Chapter' to slot together. Gilmour in the 2021 reissue liner notes:

> This, our 14th studio album, had a bit of everything, including another two chapters. There are a lot more progressive elements in the songs and also the lighter side of Saga. I remember thinking we had a strong collection of songs that covered a lot of the compositional elements that make Saga unique. We worked in LA on the album and I remember the sessions being relaxed and fun.

From my interview with Jim Crichton and from several of his online and video interviews, he sums up the album and Saga's journey so far:

> You can recognise a Saga song among thousands of others, no matter which era it's from. At the beginning of our career, we jokingly referred to our style as 'Medieval Funk', which is typical of our sense of humour. At the same time, the definition expressed the way we saw ourselves wanting to create something extraordinary. These days, we no longer need to invent terms; our band name has become a trademark in its own right. There are also a number of innovations on the album. The songs explore the respective extremes more thoroughly than ever before. The album's wide stylistic range. There are some quiet passages where we strongly rely on acoustic guitar. On the other hand, the rock passages sound heavier than before. The

> songwriting process was interrupted several times by shows in Germany and Canada, but those allowed us to transport our energy to the album.

The original CD was beautifully packaged in a book format and once again had a superb painting of 'Golden Boy' adorning the cover in a scene akin to *Images* and *Silent Knight*.

'God Knows' (5.29) (Saga)
From Mineur's 2021 reissue sleeve notes:

> 'God Knows' features all the classic Saga attributes, from Ian Crichton's unique riff and guitar solos to Jim Gilmour's frequent synchronous keyboard parts and frontman Michael Sadler's haunting melodies.

He's not wrong. Two verses and four choruses describe the brief rise and fall of the subject, Tommy, who was 'on a mission' to 'be an outlaw' who 'finally made the headlines', but was then 'lost without trace'. It begins with a slow, wistful keyboard build-up and barely audible background chatter before the track begins in earnest. The production is immaculate, crisp, bright and polished and Sadler's vocals are given prominence in the mix, ensuring his emotional delivery and lyrical nuances are clear. It's a satisfying track showcasing what's to come, with a solid drum groove, a particularly commanding snare thwack and lots of signature Saga fare. Gilmour commented that there are a lot more progressive elements on the album, particularly on this track. It became a live favourite due to its pace, intensity and rhythmic dynamism.

'The Runaway' (5.35) (Saga)
This might have made a better opener due to its high energy and brisk pace of 145 bpm. I note a change in the lyrical messaging, too, this being more contemporary, addressing a fascination/obsession with the internet and the impact and consequences that overuse can have. The words have more blatant referencing – 'smack the mouse', 'I'd better get a firewall', 'digital insanity' – and the chorus is just, 'Don't look now, I think we're on a runaway, everybody's riding on a runaway'. A short extract of a train speeding up gives way to an instrumental version of the verse melody, suitably led by Ian Crichton's phrasing. A sumptuous strutting bassline pulls the track along with intermittent 'improvised' guitar fills from the younger Crichton. This passage is classic Saga, with instrumental flourishes, mini synth and guitar leads and a key change to darken the tone, with clever use of panning to enrich the effect. It's fabulous and thankfully, this is repeated again when the excellent vocals cease. There's a lot to love about the track and when performed live, it is enthralling, with Sadler and Jim Crichton joining Gilmour on keyboards.

'Always There' (3.52) (Saga)
One of the shortest tracks on the album houses a significant amount of words, consisting of two nine-line verses and three four-line choruses, plus a short bridge. It's also one of the more introspective songs on the album, featuring heartfelt lyrics rendered by Sadler; it could be a love song or the comforting notion that there is always someone to stand by you. The acoustic guitar is simple but highly effective and the bass drum beat provides the ideal foil for the vocals, not dominant in mix level or execution. Its effectiveness is due to its simple arrangement, oozing warmth and comfort. The video can be found on *Silhouette* and the track also makes a reimagined appearance on *Symmetry.*

'Ashes To Ashes (Chapter 11)' (5.05) (Saga)
The 'Chapters' story continues, with alternating vocals between Gilmour and Sadler. The lyrics touch on the cycle of life, mortality and the eventual decay of all things, picking up from 'Not This Way' on *Full Circle*. The chorus raises the temperature and is catchy and memorable – 'Ashes to ashes and dust to dust, it all comes down to who you really trust' – followed by a distinctive guitar hook that is classic Ian Crichton and Saga, with its clean, melodic phrasing and instantly catchy motifs. The rest of the band are on form, too, opening with a suspense-building arpeggiated keyboard part, followed by dramatic shifts in tempo, intricate synth and bass passages and twin leads, with Gilmour and Crichton working in unison. A very fine track indeed, propelled by that killer lick and it, of course, appeared on *Chapters Live*, but surprisingly, no other live recording.

'Once In A Lifetime' (4.21) (Saga)
Ian Crichton dons the acoustic guitar again to strum 'Once In A Lifetime', a more positive track, being upbeat and optimistic, with a jazz-like swing pulse and an infectious sing-along chorus. It's mid-tempo and very melodic, with a terrific balance between acoustic and electric elements, highlighting Saga's skill at writing and arranging. The song is less progressive than before and more emotionally direct, which is perfect for Sadler, who is exceptional whether solo, multi-tracked, or harmonising. The lyrics reflect on rare opportunities or moments that only come once in life. There's the customary first-class guitar solo, but this is more about the song as a whole and Saga as a unit rather than individual performances. It's a breath of fresh air from some of the moodier moments on the album and would have made a great single and live choice.

'Only Human' (4.20) (Saga)
A gently picked acoustic guitar with soft synth padding opens the track and proceeds throughout, leading to Sadler almost whispering the opening lines of the chorus, his style vulnerable and introspective, as he begins a sharp

critique of humanity's imperfections whilst celebrating the resilience that comes with being who we are: 'Sometimes we come undone we're only Human, Wake up! Here comes the sun to offer us a new beginning'. The song has a steady beat and a warm and smooth pulsing bassline. The snare is quite loud and it might have blended better if it had been reduced slightly. Ian Crichton excels once more with a finely crafted lead, one of the highlights of the track, along with Sadler's melancholic and intimate tones and some minimal orchestration from the synth. It's a modest song, simple in structure with a strong message.

'That's How We Like It' (4.49) (Saga)

Gilmour is taking us back to a more contemporary theme away from love songs, sci-fi and fantasy and is now telling us what he likes: 'When we get bored we watch a war on live TV'. For context, it reminded me of The Tubes' 'TV Is King' from their 1979 album *Remote Control*. The song is playful with an upbeat tempo and catchy guitar riffs, offering a more fun and carefree feel. It illustrates the band's ability to incorporate humour and satire without sacrificing musical quality. The bass introduction sounds 'mischievous', contrasting the light and airy keyboards, heavy stabs, stellar Negus fills and a riff as heavy as anything on the album. It then all falls away for a double-tracked Gilmour to step up to sing the first verse and subsequent verses; Sadler mainly looks after the choruses. The final parts of the song reintroduce the previous musical passages with the addition of a staggering guitar solo over that monster riff. A super track of many parts that blends light and shade very neatly.

'Watching The Clock' (1.39) (Saga)

Gilmour stated that he 'got serious with the piano solo'. It's outstanding, displaying his exceptional songwriting ability and keyboard dexterity. It's a simple, short, but potent piano instrumental. A very good decision to include it on the album.

'We'll Meet Again (Chapter 15)' (5.58) (Saga)

The final 'Chapter' on the album is the penultimate one of the whole story, sitting between 'Streets Of Gold' and 'Worlds Apart', both coming soon on *Marathon*. There are also musical links to the other 'Chapters', including a quirky keyboard vamp and a colossus guitar hook for an intro that lasts for 46 seconds before the first verse, with Sadler asking, 'Have you been listening, we must have more supplies, we'll be on our way tonight' – the finale is approaching. The chorus is made memorable by its flowing melody, brilliant basslines and tight grooves. With the 'Chapters' concept coming to an end here, the lyrics perhaps outline that the aliens are about to leave but will return in the future: 'I can't tell you how, where or when, but I can tell you we'll meet again' and the telling line, 'You'll see a new light in the sky'. The instrumental section starts at 3.18, including a fine guitar solo and ends at 4.33 to a whispered chorus, that mega riff and a final chorus. It is a grandiose song with soaring vocals and intricate arrangements and is well worth seeing performed live on the *Chapters Live* and *All Areas – Live In Bonn* DVDs.

'Money Talks' (4.07) (Saga)
Saga return to the theme of money, as featured on previous albums and reflect on how life is dictated by it. It's succinctly put in the seven choruses, including the fade-out ending: 'Tell me anything that you want, 'cause we all know that money talks and we'll do exactly what it says'. However, the track starts with the four-line bridge sung acapella, which is repeated three times more. There are four verses, the final one being a repeat of the first, which is unusual for Saga. The energy of the music matches the directness of the lyrics, the verses being minimal instrumentally, but the choruses have more of a groove. There aren't any distinctive instrumental breaks or soloing, but we do get Sadler inserting phrases between the main lines of the chorus, a technique he starts to use more on subsequent albums. Gilmour noted that this track and 'Always There' were more on the 'lighter side' and that the video to support the single release, featuring Ian's children, was 'pretty funny'. The song got into the top ten in Canada but didn't trouble the European charts, even though a promotional video was shot of Saga miming to the song in a bank.

'House Of Cards' (4.20) (Saga)
It's the title track that brings the album to its conclusion and lyrically, it reminds me of 'See Them Smile' from *Images At Twilight*, focusing on material possessions. This time, it's 'best cigars', 'fastest cars', 'beluga caviar', 'Saint Tropez', 'Gucci Shoes' (directly from 'Smile') and 'silver plates'. As the title suggests, it's a story of having the finest things due to a desire for material possessions, but then it all goes wrong – 'But now your life's a mess, it took the IRS to blow it all away' – with the chorus being particularly descriptive: 'Down, down, down, down, till you bottom out'. There are elements of *Generation 13*, with a zany keyboard intro, heavy staccato riffing, fast stabbing and sinister background voices. The main groove has a pacy shuffle feel and a bobbing bass, but the verses are more 'familiar' and similar to the previous track in structure, also with minimal instrumental presence. Sadler is on top form, buoyant and confident in a song that demands changes in intensity. The break is slightly odd; it quietens the song and we hear a female voice in conversation in the distance, then a nifty lead guitar flourish, which builds up to the band playing the main motif with selected vocal extracts from the chorus. The track ends as it started, but with a chilling laughter, perhaps suggesting that the subject got their comeuppance.

Marathon (2003)

Personnel:
Ian Crichton: guitar, backing vocals
Jim Gilmour: lead keyboards, vocals
Steve Negus: drums, percussion
Michael Sadler: lead vocals, keyboards
Jim Crichton: bass, keyboards
All songs written by Saga
Recorded and mixed at Sound Image Studios, Van Nuys, California
Additional recording done at Dangling Carrot Studios, Brantford, The Blue Room, Hamilton, Good Sheppard Studios, Toronto, Canyon Studios, Malibu Canyon, California
Internet overdubs recorded using Cubase VST32 & Rocket Network
Produced by Jim Crichton
Engineered by Jim Crichton
Assistant engineers: Steve Negus, Ian Crichton, Jim Gilmour
Mixed by Jim Crichton, assisted by Michael Sadler
Front cover and inner sleeve artwork by Eric Fulghum
Photographer extraordinaire: Matthew Fried
Cover graphics and design by Penny Crichton for Picture This Productions
Running time: 51:20
Release date: 8 April 2003
Label: SPV
Highest chart places: DE: 40, CN: did not chart, US: did not chart, UK: did not chart

In 2002, activity focused on recording new material for *Marathon*. Much of the writing was done individually at home, resulting in a 'lack of cohesion' and what some described as a sterile sound, lacking atmosphere. This decision was mainly down to economics; it's much cheaper to do individual parts remotely if the equipment and technology are available. *Marathon* was composed at Crichton's apartment in Calabasas, California, on the outskirts of LA.

Sadly, it was Steve Negus' last recorded performance with the band. As a drummer and Negus fan, I remember at the time of the announcement being disappointed, but I hoped that he and the rest would make the most of their new opportunities. Ian Crichton in the 2021 reissue liner notes:

> This record finishes the 'Chapters' which started on our first release. It was also the last record with Steve Negus, our original drummer. At this point in our career, we thought we'd run a marathon, having started in the late 1970s.

Jim Crichton:

> The songs on *Marathon* continue stylistically what had characterised *Full Circle*, *House Of Cards*, and, at the end of the day, the most successful

> releases of our career. There's no experimenting with different stylistic elements the way we'd done with *Generation 13* and *Pleasure And The Pain.*

Following *Marathon*'s release, Saga embarked on an extensive tour presenting not only their greatest hits, but also tracks from the new album. Martin Popoff, in an interview with Michael Sadler in July 2002, asked: 'You are coming here with *Jethro Tull*, is that part of the tour? In response, Sadler said:

> No, we're just doing limited shows this year in honour of the 25th anniversary. Because the new CD will be out soon, *Marathon*, which we're working on right now. I think there's a bit of every CD we've done in these songs, but we also keep trying to keep our ears open as to what's going around us, without being directly influenced by anything specifically. So I can't say whether there's any kind of change in the sound, but perhaps with *House Of Cards* there are a few moments that get really intricate, sort of back to our trickier days.

Popoff also spoke to Jim Crichton in August 2002: 'To me, the new album is just a continuation of the last two and sounds very similar sonically. Nothing really new, short of Daryl using a guitar processor on some of his melody keyboards, just to crap them out a bit.'

Saga celebrated their 25th anniversary by playing a one-off open-air show in Bonn in the summer of 2002, filmed for the *All Areas DVD*.

Two years had passed since *House Of Cards* and four years since *Full Circle*; along with these previous albums, *Marathon* is the last album of this trio to offer a similar musical experience. The production is also very similar to the other two in the 'series', immaculate, clean, vibrant and extremely well balanced.

'Marathon' (4.59) (Saga)

With this opening track, I noticed that, if anything, the snare is less prominent than on *House Of Cards*, but sonically, everything else appears to be the same. A strident bass and playful toms open up, swiftly joined by the verse melody played on guitar, also used for the instrumental break later in the song. It's the chorus that appears first, with solid chugging guitar as the main foundation. Sadler then appears for the first verse and sounds great: 'It takes time to get to Avalon, That's why we're on this Marathon', Avalon being the mythical island featured in the Arthurian legend. The song, therefore, relates to endurance and perseverance, using the metaphor of running a marathon to describe pushing through life's challenges, staying determined and keeping focused on the journey. There are plenty of words across the verses and bridge, some lower down in the mix to change the dynamic and Sadler also adds to this with frequent ad-libs across the track. It wouldn't be Saga without the tight, solid stabs to begin the instrumental segment, starring a short but spectacular guitar solo. A reassuring, solid track and a suitable album opener. It would seem all is well.

'How Are You?' (5.22) (Saga)

There's a more laid-back and conversational tone to this number in which the narrator is talking to the protagonist about their attitude and behaviour and warning them that they must be more positive and take responsibility for their actions. It features ambient keyboard pads and sultry fingerstyle bass patterns. The verse is the calmest section of the song, being mainly vocal-led with a warmer, deeper bass presence and there's a well-constructed guitar phrase that links the verses and chorus, a typical Ian Crichton creation. Everything comes to life when the chorus appears, which is just a simple repeat of 'how are ya feelin' now?' complemented by a mighty guitar riff and a spirited rhythm. The introduction returns for the middle eight, with some deft guitar textures and smooth accents, before the tempo increases for the guitar solo that weaves its way majestically across the track. This fairly lengthy section at 1:46 has an improvised element, adding to the adventurous nature of the track, with some chops from Crichton I'd not really heard previously. A well-constructed song performed proficiently, with a magnificent instrumental section. Gilmour remarked that this track in particular was an instant audience favourite. It did appear on the *Marathon World Tour 2003 (The Official Bootleg)*.

'Breathing Lessons' (4.24) (Saga)

Jim Crichton wrote the lyrics for Sadler for this sensitive ballad. Gilmour thought at the time 'that this is a fantastic number that should have been a hit by rights.' There are some obvious rhymes – 'heaven' and 'seven', 'weather' and 'leather' – but also more thought-provoking lines: 'But I've seen you in lace and leather and I keep that to myself' and 'I know how to live on credit, take a dive & never regret it'. The narrator justifies the need for breathing lessons, recognising that they could be pushing too hard in aspects of their life and need the support of another to help them to stay grounded and focus on what's important. Keen observers will note references to previous Saga songs within the lyrics – 'Compromise(s)', 'Shake The Tree', 'Climb The Ladder' – a neat technique that they continued to use throughout their albums. Musically, the track as a whole is sumptuous as it weaves through the various lyrical transitions with a constantly engaging synthesiser refrain, multi-tracked vocals on the verses and a tender electronic pulse for the rhythm, with an occasional guitar fill. No solos, no change in dynamics, just a delightful song enabling Sadler to be at his most soulful. I agree with Gilmour.

'Hands Up' (3.44) (Saga)

Saga return to a more pop-rock style, but it's still a step up, with strong guitar riffs and synth ostinatos in abundance, as well as forceful vocals that are multi-tracked and harmonised, perhaps slightly overdone. There's a heck of a lot going on underneath the vocals, with some exquisite instrumentation and changes in rhythmic patterns and dynamics and I'll bet it was interesting writing, arranging and recording the various elements. The verses, choruses and bridge take it up to 2.07, then it's time for the instrumental break, which is made up of a super guitar riff, forceful bass drum patterns locked into solid basslines to anchor the melody, a searing guitar solo and a lovely double synth pattern, which reminded me of 'Blinded By The Light' by Manfred Mann. It's an impressive track all round and I'd say it's Negus's best performance on the album, with some marvellous drumming. The words are possibly a rallying call to take action or make a stand: 'Hands up get in line, it's time to step into the light, hands up wait for the sign, we're gonna raise the roof tonight'.

'Streets Of Gold (Chapter 14)' (5.11) (Saga)

The first 'Chapter' song on *Marathon* features a distinctive Saga vocal performance with Sadler and Gilmour alternating lines in a call and response: Gilmour: 'Please stop', Sadler: 'We can't do that', Gilmour: 'Why not?', Sadler: 'We've done the math' and so on. In the context of the story, my feeling is that this is a conversation between Einstein and the aliens. This back-and-forth dialogue is an unusual approach to a song and without the 'Chapter' context, it probably wouldn't work as well. I'm not sure if the lyrics provide additional pieces for the 'jigsaw', but there are Saga song titles to discover (at least four, I think). The track itself starts with warm, hypnotic synth pads, then a signature Ian Crichton guitar hook to lead into the vocals. The chorus is very strong in melody and words and picks up the pace, adding intensity. Halfway through the song, the solo kicks in; Crichton is initially reserved but builds to some exceptional runs in this fairly long section to prepare for the vocal bridge, soothingly sung by Sadler and Gilmour. The last verse has Sadler in role, sounding more desperate, before the song dissolves during the final chorus. A magnificent on-stage version can be heard on *Chapters Live*.

'The Blind Side Of Your Heart' (4.35) (Saga)

It's Gilmour that begins with a delicate, almost sentimental synthesiser sequence for this ballad and love song, coaxing in Sadler, who is exceptionally adept at ballads, portraying the character in this song with soulfulness and serenity. It would be reasonable to believe that these are his own words based on the subject matter and his lyrical approach to previous songs. The track's melody matches the sentiment with a soothing bass undercurrent and what sounds like a drum machine pulsing the gentle heartbeat rhythm. It could be 'proper' drums just played in this style with subtle cross-sticking, but there are no fills, indicating it's more likely to be the former. The song seems to delve into vulnerability and emotional blind spots people have in relationships: 'Let it out there's no doubt you'd be better off without the blind side of your heart'. It's a pleasant enough track with some fine harmonies in the chorus, a hint of acoustic guitar and a more laid-back but still entertaining lead guitar. It could easily have been a single.

'Return To Forever' (4.26) (Saga)
Back to a more conventional Saga and straight in with a pacy groove at 136 bpm, a guitar-driven melody, a combination of solid riffing and a signature lead motif. The verses have urgency, with vocal responses to the main lines much lower in the mix and effects-laden. The same arrangement is also used during the choruses: 'Touching the untouchable, it's always a big surprise and when you're walking with your pockets full, you can enjoy the ride'. There is the customary change in dynamic, where most of the instruments drop out, followed by exquisite, rapid stabbing as a precursor to the lead guitar, which is another gem. The words are a self-reflection, questioning assistance and purpose perhaps, but with an answer: 'I found a way to return to forever, back to the days when I had nothing to lose'. I like the song a lot because of the tempo, vocal and instrumental arrangements, the bass guitar's rhythmic backbone and the top-notch production. It's simple in structure, but a substantial rock song.

'Too Deep' (4.35) (Saga)
I'd sum this song up as a combination of what's gone before on the album, following a similar structure to the previous track in particular and containing musical elements from the others. There's almost a repeat of the call and response vocal technique, but this time it's predominantly Sadler singing both parts. The chorus in particular is a real strength; it's well-constructed and skilfully sung across several ranges and the instrumentation adopts the Saga formula of fabulous twin hooks and individual solo efforts by both guitar and keyboards. These are impressive in their own right, but outstanding when blended together. Rhythmically, Crichton and Negus work well in tandem, keeping it fairly straightforward. The well-written and observed lyrics revolve around being overwhelmed by emotions, circumstances, or life's challenges: 'Too deep for the tears, you left me waiting here, just frozen in fear, those cold uncertain times'. Other highlights of the track include the twin lead during breaks and the effective use of both speakers to highlight the phrasing. It's a good song with its own intensity and character, but perhaps not different enough to make it really stand out.

'You Know I Know (Chapter 12)' (4.19)
This is a big song, heavy on guitars and more obvious lyrically in relation to the album-spanning 'Chapters' story. 'You Know I Know' is a credible title, pointing towards the forthcoming 'Chapters' conclusion, the final track on this album. There's a recognition, 'you know I know', that everything has fallen

apart, 'nothing remains of what we knew', but there's a decision to rebuild, 'so now the task of reconstruction' and to 'prepare for the future'. The aliens are not giving up. The vocals are recited in a call-and-response pattern again and as with 'Streets Of Gold', which is cleverly cited in the song, there's a conversation underway, this time perhaps between two aliens. There are also more references to previous Saga songs, most notably 'No Regrets'. Crichton's solo is arguably his best on the album, starting as a melodious link between the verse and chorus, before developing into much more, with some rapid-fire arpeggios, finely executed shredding and softer runs as the climate lightens. Guitar chugging takes us to the next segment, incorporating short but magical synth lines before the vocals continue to the end. For the next instalment, go to 'Uncle Albert's Eyes'.

'Rise And Shine' (3.32) (Saga)
Uncertainty and disappointment abound on this track – 'Anxious bride, but still no sign of the groom' – but despite the missed chances, there's still time to grasp any opportunities: 'Rise and Shine or yesterday will slip into tomorrow'. A resonant acoustic guitar unwraps the track, soon met by vocals and a drum machine effect, so it's very experimental at this stage. The 'bass drum' accents in particular pop and bounce along with a controlled freedom. The vocals in the verse are lower down and slightly muffled; the chorus, however, is more open and clear and therefore, to me, more appealing. Due to the lack of a backbeat, there's a melodic flow with haunting keyboard overtones and calming vocal harmonies. A lead guitar solo is executed during an instrumental version of the chorus, its restrained sound suiting this innovative approach to the track. Saga have a distinct style, but they are fearless of the unorthodox, as evidenced in their 1990s output. This is a further example of the intent to try new things, such as the unusual vocal phrasing, irregular song structure and use of the drum machine. It does take a few listens to be fully convinced. It was released as a single with the B-side 'Hands Up'.

'Worlds Apart (Chapter 16)' (6.10) (Saga)
It's 'Chapter 16', the very last one in the concept, the end of an era, which means no more aliens to adorn the album covers and no more pieces of the jigsaw to decipher. Typically, Saga choose the title of their most successful album to date as the name for the final chapter. Mineur describes the track as 'the most unusual song' and Jim Crichton himself explained to me during an interview that...

> ...this six-minute number is split into two stylistically tonally different sections. At the same time, together with the title song, it's the toughest track on the whole album. But as usual, fans of quieter, more straightforward directives get their money's worth.

Jim Gilmour has the privilege of delivering the opening lines, 'why do we do, what we do now and what should we do', sung in choral tones accompanied by a church-organ-like synth. Sadler questions, 'Would you like a new start that would be worlds apart?' The track then proceeds with a conventional mid-tempo rock groove right in the pocket, with an exemplary guitar riff, supplementary lead guitar and synth harmonies following each line. The passages are quite similar in style, but there's just enough contrast between the verse, chorus and bridge to keep the track absorbing vocally and the extended instrumental sections allow all the musicians to flaunt their abilities. Sadler's keyboard prowess and Gilmour's phenomenal ability to play two keyboards at once when on stage can be seen on *Marathon World Tour 2003: The Official Bootleg*. For this track, a multi-layered repetition of the intro starts the final countdown with one minute to go. The end: 'Would you like a new start? Worlds apart'. Does the 'Chapters' story make sense now? No. Did it achieve what it intended? Most likely.

Phase One (2003)

Personnel:
Michael Sadler: lead vocal, keyboard, Moog
Jim Crichton: bass guitar, Moog bass
Greg Chadd: keyboards, vocals, vocoder, Moog
Ian Crichton: acoustic, electric guitars
Steve Negus: drums, percussion
Recorded at Phase One Studios, Toronto, Canada, 1978
Originally recorded by Paul Gross
Produced by Paul Gross
Additional mastering: Darcy Scott, Noise Floor Studios
Running time: 53:37
Release date: 20 May 2003
Label: SPV
Highest chart places: did not chart in any territory

During the *Pleasure And The Pain* era, the unexpected *Phase One* was released on CD as a homage to the recording studio used for the first three albums. It was initially sold as a special limited edition at gigs and to Saga club members only, containing demos from the early recordings and some previously unheard material. Not surprisingly, the first presses soon sold out, so this second reissue, a remastered version, appeared much later.

Its booklet states, 'What one hears is the band in the studio playing live, taking some new songs for a test drive.' It also explained that *Phase One* was originally released during the 1997 world tour, containing three demo versions of songs from *Images At Twilight,* which aren't remixed or dubbed, with five new, previously unreleased songs. It does sound like *Images* and the production from Gross is great, even the rough mixes. Within the 'scribbled' notes inside the booklet, Jim Crichton is described as 'Tape Librarian' and Penny Crichton as 'Photo Librarian'. Jim Crichton explained in the CD booklet:

> These are demo tapes we found of songs we were trying out for the second album; some didn't appear on *Images At Twilight*. What you will hear is the band in the studio playing live, taking some new songs for a test drive. I hope you enjoy the other second album.

This is an album from out of the blue, but it's a welcome surprise and it's refreshing to return to the past to compare the sound, performance and songwriting with the band's later offerings. The difference in style, tone, instrumentation and musicality is astonishing. The most obvious examples are the melodies being more synth-based and Sadler's use of an alternate vocal technique. It's a couple of years prior to him working with Rupert Hine and his infamous insistence to disregard the choral style and to adopt a more 'mature' delivery whilst recording *Worlds Apart*. It's also great to hear Paul Gross' production again, too, specifically on the songs that didn't make it onto *Images*.

'Half The Time' 7:06 (Saga)
'Half The Time' sums up Sadler's choral background, enthusiastic youthfulness and relative inexperience beautifully and he is loud in the mix. It's a fairly complex song, experimental and playful and it does sound like a well-executed demo with plenty of vocal and instrumental twists and turns and tempo changes, but listen out for Jim Crichton's bass patterns; they're a treat, as are the customary stabs and accenting between the vocal passages. For Saga, this is a long song, possibly relying heavily on improvisation, although it really ends 30 seconds before the seven minutes are up. It appears as though the band were finding their feet, including Gross and embracing the opportunity to impress. As a result, it does appear to be a jam session incorporating everyone's ideas converted into a song. There's no lyric sheet, but it's another 'Time' track and clearly not considered good enough to make it onto *Images*, but I like it.

'Old Man' 4:29 (Saga)
It's a frisky, light-hearted introduction, with twin keyboard and guitar spearheading the main melody at a fairly rapid pace, reminding me of early Styx. The verse is respectable enough, but the chorus is exceptional and features a great lyric: 'Old Man won't you teach me your magic; I'd like to see the world the same way as you', the protagonist wishing for the old man to impart his wisdom. There are signs that the band are developing their musical chops, with a very proficient lead guitar solo and some absorbing synth and piano flourishes by Greg Chadd throughout. It is a more complete track than 'Half The Time' and the instrumental ending is fabulous, even though the finale, with its stabbed phrasing, is a bit obvious and twee. It's my favourite of the previously 'unheard' tracks.

'Hangman' 7:48 (Saga)
The longest track on the album and the one with possibly the strangest title and theme. It begins with swirling synths and improvised impish keyboard lilts that last for 1:34 (far too long) before a thumping kick drum, Moog and off-beat cymbal strokes, turning to a muted crash, build the tension. Things are starting to get darker at 2.17 with the most sorrowful vocals: 'Soon those footsteps will be coming here to rescue me'. The second verse explains that the subject shot someone whilst they were drunk and in the chorus, they are appealing to the hangman to make it quick and painless. The music matches the desperate words and it's all a bit sombre and laboured. The playing is pretty good, though; the piano and bass figures work well with the overall melody and rhythm, leading to a colossal ending, with bombastic instrumentation that's very prog, concluding with a tight snare roll from

Negus and a short snare solo, presumably signalling the final act. The track is experimental and much too long, possibly one of the reasons why it wasn't chosen for *Images*. It would have stood out a mile against more upbeat and positive tracks that were included. However, it's definitely worth showcasing on this bonus album, but for Saga fans only, I'd suggest, as it's not the best representation of the band.

'You're Not Alone' (Demo Version) 5:37 (Saga)
This is very similar to the original but with more pace and urgency. The vocal and second harmonies in the verse don't sit as well and the chorus in particular has slightly different vocal articulation and expressions that are hard to get used to. Some of the accenting is misplaced and too loud and the guitar solo at the end is drowned by shouts of the song title. This is me being fussy and only because I'm used to the final version. It's an acceptable precursor, though and as a demo, it doesn't get much better in performance and production and thus didn't need too much tweaking to get it to the supreme track it ended up being.

'Mouse In A Maze' (Demo Version) 5:44 (Saga)
The comments I made about the previous track could also be attributed to this version of 'Mouse In A Maze'. It's got that demo quality, mainly due to the mix and not the playing, but even in this form, it's fabulous and worthy of repeated listens to better understand the evolution of the track and *Images At Twilight* as a whole. The production is raw, crisp and edgy, which I quite like and overall, the track is a fine comparison to the finished article, with only a few slight differences, such as the micro drum role in the introduction and the more prominent vocal harmonies. Despite these details, everything is roughly the same vocally, even with the trickier instrumental elements, so it's a great reminder of what exemplary musicians Saga were, even then.

'Don't Bother' 4:04 (Saga)
The shortest track on the album and without doubt the oddest and possibly the most bizarre track Saga have ever done. It sounds like a recording of a rehearsal, in which lyrics were added later. It's a quirky number in 2/4 time at 170 bpm in the main, so briskly done in a vaudeville style with a megaphone for the vocal effect. It is solid, tight and extremely well executed and it would appear they had fun doing it. The driving force is the excellent bluesy bass guitar and the gliding synth refrains; there's also a credible keyboard solo from Chadd, but I wouldn't have thought the track was a favourite of Ian Crichton's, with the limited opportunity on offer to insert an appropriate guitar solo.

'Hot To Cold' (Demo Version) 5:40 (Saga)
This is a reminder of just how intricate the arrangements were in the early days of Saga and it's still staggering to me that this was a track that featured

on only their second album, some 25 years previously – it has absolutely stood the test of time. This wasn't their most successful track in relation to critical acclaim, fan favourites, or obvious choices for live outings or 'greatest hits' appearances. However, it's a superbly constructed song, masterfully played and this particular version is another wonderful, vigorous and dynamic 'demo'. However, there are substantial differences, including more guitar picking, Chadd's vocals lines being more prominent and improvised and the missing first lines of the choruses, which is unnerving, so I'm glad that they corrected that. The strange and abrupt ending just doesn't work, either, but the synths are bombastic and the subtle key changes add greater energy to a marvellous song.

'Don't Step Out Of Line' (Saga) 5:20

The tightly synchronised bass and drum pattern intro could well have come from Saga's Canadian peers, Max Webster. It's got the melody from 'America's Veins' (*High Class In Borrowed Shoes,* 1975) and the hook of 'Blue River Liquor Shine' (*Universal Juveniles,* 1980), which came two years later. The track proceeds for 1.13 until there's a complete change of tune from a quirky, punchy, off-beat instrumental to a faster, more flowing synth-led passage before the vocals arrive. It's a segway that may well have been pieced together in the control room. The verse is a plain affair and the chorus is just a mediocre one-line repeat of the track's title. There are some commendable elements instrumentally, particularly the introduction, but the arrangement isn't up to the usual standard and the song just isn't that good. Let us not forget, though, that this was just a demo.

The bonus track is 'You're Not Alone (Live)'. It's the *Pleasure And The Pain* version lifted directly from *Detours Live.*

Network (2004)

Personnel:
Michael Sadler: vocals
Jim Crichton: bass
Ian Crichton: guitar
Jim Gilmour: keyboards, vocals
Christian Simpson: drums
All songs written by Saga
Recorded and mixed at Sound Image Studios, Van Nuys, California
Additional recording done at Dangling Carrot Studios, Brantford, Good Sheppard Studios, Toronto, Canyon Studios, Malibu Canyon
Produced by Jim Crichton
Engineered by Jim Crichton
Mixed by Jim Crichton, assisted by Michael Sadler
Cover concept: Jim Crichton
Cover design by Penny Crichton for Imagestockaid
Running time: 49:51
Release date: 30 September 2004
Label: SPV
Highest chart places: DE: 78, CN: did not chart, US: did not chart, UK: did not chart

When Steve Negus left Saga on 20 June 2003, he published an open letter on his website. He felt that he could no longer function within the present framework and it was time for him to pursue new ventures. He emphasised that after 26 years of playing together, it was not an easy decision, not based on any major disagreements, but more about external circumstances beyond his control. He wished the rest of the band well and knew that they would remain friends. He also thanked the fans for their support.

He played his final show in Hamilton on 12 July 2003. Gilmour: 'Steve asked us for an extended hiatus. He simply needed more time to himself and his private life. Naturally, we didn't place any obstacles in his way. Steve knew that he was welcome to return at any time and that we'd greet him with open arms.' With Negus's departure, the search was on for a new drummer and following extensive auditions, Christian Simpson was selected and settled in well.

Network was released in 2004 and was well-received with some great reviews and as a result, the subsequent tour in November 2004 quickly sold out. Progressiveworld.net announced, 'This is Saga's most modern-sounding album. The songwriting is impeccable.' They further enthused about the instrumentation, poignant bass punches, luscious piano, guitar technique and intelligently integrated sound bites. The approach to recording also helped; unlike *Marathon,* the previous album, the band worked together in the same room, with no parts being downloaded.

Martin Popoff interviewed Jim Crichton in November 2005 and asked, 'Musically, where does *Network* fit?'

> It's a fairly punchy, heavy album. I think it's kind of retro-Saga with an edge. Hopefully, it's fresh-sounding and it has all the classic Saga ingredients. We actually recorded it live, with analogue tape. So we did the old-fashioned, old-school way. We just played live and whatever needed to be cleaned up, we cleaned it up and overdubbed if required. So it's not like live completely, but we went in and counted 1, 2, 3, 4 and played something, which is unusual these days. Normally, people chop the songs up into bits and pieces and all kinds of craziness.

Network's tour sticker on the original CD release shows a start date of 31 October 2004 at the Mean Fiddler in London, ending 25 gigs later on New Year's Eve at Villingen in Germany.

It was a 17-month turnaround from *Marathon*, but some familiar attributes remained, including Jim Crichton as the engineer and producer, although some additional recordings came from three other studios in Ontario and California. The major difference from the previous album being new drummer, Christian Simpson, replacing Steve Negus. The album's theme, hence, the 'Channel' prefixed to each track, is TV and film viewed through a nostalgic lens.

'Channel 1. On The Air' (6.30) (Saga)

What sounds like Sam from *Generation 13* announces 'You are watching FNN' over a smooth, bouncy keyboard melody and Sadler informs, 'We're on the air tonight', just prior to a pre-verse build-up. The verse itself is at a surprisingly leisurely pace for an opening track, with the vocals well up in the mix. The bridge is mainly vocals the first time around, with the word 'extrapolate' used to rhyme with 'don't be late', so with the latter, Saga are back to including previous song titles in their lyrics. It's all fairly sedate until the chorus bursts through with a dramatic change of emphasis. The instruments are 'turned up' and it's recognisable Saga, driven by heavy riffing guitars, complementary keyboard refrains and forceful vocals. There's still room for a subtle piano and at 3.30, Simpson introduces himself with a nifty little drum solo. Sadler himself claims this to be 'a very Saga song'; with a diverse range of instrumental sections, cunning momentum changes and some top-notch performances, including Simpson with some tasty fills. He isn't wrong. It's a grand song, but the production doesn't have the same warmth and precision as the last three albums, being more rough and gritty. When played live, the opening tricks the audience into thinking it's going to be 'Don't Be Late'.

'Channel 2. Keep It Reel' (4.22) (Saga)

It's a smart use of the word 'Reel' in the context of the broadcasting theme. Lyrically, this appears to be a joint effort with a mix of both Sadler and Jim

Crichton's style: conversational, advisory and with a touch of fantasy. It begins with the line 'Of all the deeds of daring-do, you think the daring dare to dream', a reference to heroic adventures and a selection of words that are more obvious pointers to the theme of being pulled into media and entertainment, mainly TV and film. There's a nostalgia trip activated by a radio voice introduction, swift hand-tapping arpeggios from Ian Crichton and a jittery, accented, heavy transition into the first verse. It's a good pace, with energetic riffing under the melody and a loud metallic thwack of the snare. At 2.31, Crichton demonstrates his virtuosity with a series of marvellous Van Halen-esque runs. More of the same basic structure follows – verse, chorus, bridge – before the track comes to a dead stop. It's a solid, well-played rock number, but again suffers a tad from an overall abrasive tone.

'Channel 3. I'm Back' (5.04) (Saga)

In conventional Saga style, there are three different segments in the first 40 seconds of the track, starting with a moderate build-up of playful synths, an upbeat chorus melody and a short call and response between keyboards and guitar, alternating between speakers. The verse is sung with short, detached notes and the bridge features a chant of 'I'm back' four times. The chorus is smoother and more melodic, with Sadler's appeal, 'Bring on the rain, clear my eyes, so I can start again'. This chorus is repeated several times and along with the bridge forms the majority of the song, delivered at full pelt or as a more gentle interpretation. Sadler's is excellent in both styles, showcasing his versatility and range. There are no particular standout elements from any musician; Crichton's solo is, as usual, noteworthy, if a tad quiet, with a supportive rhythm section blended nicely in the background. There's nothing too impactful; it's just a well-executed song and a solid band performance.

'Channel 4. If I Were You' (3.53) (Saga)

This opens with an enchanting acoustic guitar and sympathetic synth padding that contrasts well in tone and energy with the previous 'Channel 3'. Sadler's harmonious vocals arrive in no time for this love song's verse: 'I've been told the heart is fragile at the best of times, but how much pain should we endure?'. The rest of the band join in for the chorus, which has a charming, laid-back groove and tasteful harmonies, a suitable backdrop for the positive, advisory theme: 'If I were you I'd disregard the past, remember what they say the sun will one day re-appear'. At 2.20, the instrumental passage allows Gilmour a short, delicate keyboard solo before the catchy chorus returns to fade out. It's a good song, showcasing Saga's ability to create emotional ballads, playing very much to one of Sadler's strengths.

'Channel 5. Outside Looking In' (4.20) (Saga)

This is a chorus-led track, sung five times in total. The song commences with Sadler: 'As the world turns I've got a front row seat and a guiding light is watching over me'. The instrumental break has some exquisite soundscapes and a touch of The Beatles (*Sgt. Pepper*), dominated by the Mellotron and the verses are mainly Sadler singing across some charming synthesiser phrases, percussive flourishes and serene basslines. It's a respectable enough track with sufficient changes in texture and the Crichtons and Gilmour offering inventive support to the vocals. There's no guitar solo, but that's fine, as the track works well as is.

'Channel 6. Don't Look Now' (5.11) (Saga)
Gilmour's classy, expressive piano opening prefaces a short, distinctive Saga sequence incorporating quick, tight rhythmic patterns. Vocals are multi-tracked, adding depth and in typical Saga style, Ian Crichton adds a heavy riffed motif at the end of each line. It's a stellar chorus, perhaps the most melodic on the album, because of the sustained last notes. 'Don't look now, just come and get, what are you waiting for?' is the opening gambit and this changes each time round as the song progresses. The first round of vocals is completed at 2.19, permitting Crichton to riff enthusiastically to the opening sequence as a precursor to the instrumental section, where he switches roles to lead guitarist to execute another staggering display of soloing. The chap is quite brilliant at incorporating a wide range of impressive techniques and so is Gilmour, who sits back down at the piano for an extended repeat of the track's opening. Lyrically, it appears it's still on the broadcast theme: 'What's in the mirror, can you see you? Can't let the lighting deceive you. Here's your chance, don't you waste it'. So, make the most of your screen opportunity. Another very likeable song.

'Channel 7. Live At Five' (5:23) (Saga)
'Live At Five' appears to be the title of a TV news show, reflected in the three main segments of the song: the first verse ('We are working on it every day, to fill you full of doubt'), the bridge ('Now we're live at five and we'll be here all night') and the chorus ('If you need some good news, you'll have to wait until we're through, coz this isn't life, it's live at five'). Of the three segments, the chorus is the most outward critique of the media and news reporting, aided by the slight air of sarcasm and frustration in Sadler's vocal approach. Musically, most prominent are the short, sharp guitar riffs, rumbling bass guitar and Ian Crichton's simple hook, sitting neatly between each of the verses. The tempo is a very steady 127 bpm throughout, allowing Simpson to build on the groove with tom and bass drum chops as the track progresses. Another likeable track with a strong, infectious chorus.

'Channel 8. Back Where We Started' (4:21) (Saga)
It's Gilmour's turn to be in the spotlight, sustaining chords on his synth, supplemented by Jim Crichton's smooth walking bass. The first part of the first verse is mellow, with Simpson initially cross-sticking a polyrhythm as

Gilmour sings in his distinctive tones, not unlike Jon Anderson of Yes. The engaging chorus chants 'Round, round, we're just back where we started', but it's not until the second verse – and the mention of the 'media machine' – that the theme becomes clearer, indicating where the locus of control lies. There's a brief but welcome keyboard solo during the middle eight before the track begins to fade on the chorus. A pretty good track that would have benefited from a bit more dynamism.

'Channel 9. Believe' (5.00) (Saga)

The track opens with Gilmour on piano, producing smooth legato notes that remind me of the intro to UFO's classic 'Doctor, Doctor'. The similarity ends there. Instead of Michael Schenker blasting out the legendary lead hook, Michael Sadler caresses our ears with a soft, almost whispered lyric – 'Talk to me, tell me how it feels to be misunderstood' – accompanied only by the piano. And so it continues for 2:40, until all the words have been expressed. Simpson brings the band in with crisp, complex fills to a full band repeat of the piano melody, complete with soaring synths as Sadler emotionally and dramatically hits the higher notes perfectly – his finest moment on the album. Crichton takes over for a while, rendering an emotive lead to which the track fades out. A fitting climax to a powerful song about holding onto faith.

'Channel 10. Don't Make A Sound' (6.23)

A gentle, intriguing and mysterious keyboard intro soon turns more menacing when the vocals, pulsating bass and heartbeat rhythm take hold for the first two verses. The next verse is more intense, with the even-paced strut of the pulse, before a melodic and memorable three-line bridge with the same momentum. Bang on three minutes, Simpson's flair is unleashed as he flies around the toms before setting a slower, more deliberate groove for the next bridge. At 4.02, it's as though another song has been seamlessly sewn on, consisting of staggered syncopated beats across the toms, almost military in their execution, coordinated with a sharp, staccato vocal delivery. At 4.56, there's a dramatic, high-octane change as the tempo accelerates for a short period, allowing Crichton (to the left) and Gilmour (to the right) to solo independently. It's a powerful end to a mighty fine album, but I'm left still pining for more clarity and warmth overall.

Trust (2006)

Personnel:
Michael Sadler: lead vocals, keyboards
Jim Crichton: bass, keyboards
Jim Gilmour: lead keyboards, vocals
Ian Crichton: guitars
Brian Doerner: drums
Recorded at Fantom Finger Studios, Ontario
All songs recorded and engineered by Saga, Geoff Kent and Marc Scola
Mixed by Geoff Kent, Ian Crichton and Andi Charal
All songs produced by Saga, co-produced by Geoff Kent
DVD recorded and edited by Mike Filsinger
Artwork: Balázs Papáy
Running time 49:46
Release date: 21 April 2006
Label: Inside Out
Highest chart places: DE: 23, CN: did not chart, US: did not chart, UK: did not chart

In 2005, due to a medical condition affecting his coordination, Simpson could no longer play the drums and sadly had to leave the band. A replacement was found relatively quickly in former Helix drummer Brian Doerner via a mutual friend of Jim Gilmour's. Helix and Saga formed around the same time, so Doerner was well aware of the band. He made his debut in 2005 on a live Canadian TV broadcast, followed by a European tour, where he performed the signature drum passages created by Negus.

Plans for the next album began and it was agreed to use a different studio to enable Jim Crichton to focus on writing and performing rather than production. Saga returned to Canada to Metalworks Studio in Mississauga, owned by Gil Moore of Triumph, to mix the tracks. The studio manager was none other than Paul Gross, who was asked to aid proceedings and offer his opinion. The album sold reasonably well, with fans enjoying a 'return to form' and continuing to buy albums and attend gigs. Regarding the record, Sadler explained to Ammerlaan:

> Apart from having one of my favourite album covers, this record contains and showcases so much of the musicality of the band. I love the diversity of the songs and it presents a wide enough spectrum of the band's notable trademarks to give a first-time listener a fairly accurate sense of what Saga is all about. I find it to be a very positive-feeling album and it contains two of my favourite tracks.

A sticker within the original CD provides details of the *Trust World Tour* in 2006, listing 30 dates from 18 April to 24 May, starting in Nuremberg and ending in London. The 'special edition' double digipack CD was superbly presented and came with a *The Making Of Trust* DVD, which should have been much better and didn't really do what it said on the 'tin'. I was expecting and wanted more about the creation of the songs and the arrangement and recording processes, which unfortunately didn't materialise. Still, better than nothing.

Unusually, the members of Saga aren't attributed to particular instruments on these liner notes, so there are some unknowns and therefore, I've included educated assumptions in my analysis of the tracks.

'That's As Far As I'll Go' (4.36) (Saga)

Right from the first synthesiser note, you can feel the energy and freshness and when Sadler comes sweeping in with the vocals, there is definitely a renewed vigour and enthusiasm since *Network* two years previously. The production is much better, too, crisp, rich, natural and modern. This is all exciting stuff and it's only been the first 20 seconds. What is clear is the presence of new drummer Brian Doerner and his approach to rhythms, fills and the sound of his kit. He's fluent, with some tasteful bass drum patterns in particular, but he just keeps it simple and tight.

Track one has intent and focus across the different sections, with the main melody coming from synthesisers. The strongest section is the chorus, an uplifting sing-along: 'You know all you need to know, that's as far as I will go'. It will stay with you for a while. The instrumental break is vibrant and orchestral, concluding with a brief but marvellous Ian Crichton guitar outburst; he certainly is on form. It's a cracking start to the album. A highly recommended live version can be seen and heard on *Contact Live In Munich*.

'Back To The Shadows' (5.16) (Saga)

Layered synthesisers create a harmonious, expectant opening that continues into the first verse, which has an easy pop-rock tempo. There's a minimalistic, speak-singing approach to the vocals and a silky synth and guitar sequence follows each line. The verse proceeds with 'How do you do?, We've all been looking for you, you didn't give us a clue'. The dynamics increase for the bridge, with Saga adopting their distinctive call and response: 'forget about it', 'you can't see me'. The chorus also packs a punch, with a complimentary melody and lyrics that reference 'time', 'fading away' and 'it's back to the shadows'. Scrutinising the words doesn't help too much; it's not a story and it's not particularly reflective, advisory, or indeed very pleasant: 'please go away, cos you've got nothing to say'. On occasions, backing is sprightly and grandiose, with guitar and synthesiser working in tandem. There's a magnificently lush solo from Gilmour and I can hear elements of Saga's earliest albums, including superlative twin leads, which is satisfying and reminiscent of the band at their captivating best.

'I'm OK' (5.36) (Saga)
The tempo reduces from the previous number for this finely crafted and tender track, which welcomes the first verse after an energetic opening of instrumental stabs and elegant fills from Doerner. This is the best start to a song on the album and its theme seems to deal with internal conflict and creating a space to develop inner strength: 'Some days are like all the rest, for all the wrong reasons'. At the bridge, Sadler announces that he 'didn't mean to start the fire, how was I to know', in keeping with the continued internal discussion about his own wellbeing. In the chorus, we are treated to a 13-year-old reference: 'secure in my illusion'. The song is also very strong instrumentally, with excellent piano refrains and synth padding and the guitar phrasing during the chorus is classic Crichton, demonstrating a lively journey up and down the fretboard. At four minutes precisely, it all changes to a heavier riff-driven segment, with the keyboard meandering expertly in the background and Jim Crichton and Doerner clearly enjoying each other's company. In a live setting, the former can be seen rotating his Moog and it's very entertaining.

'Time To Play' (3.31) (Saga)
This number has a basic song structure, with just a verse and chorus and it's done and dusted fairly quickly. It starts with an intriguing guitar motif, leading into the first verse, which is repeated further into the song. It's a sound and style that reminded me of Mr Mister's 1987 album *Go On*, in that it has a soulful, bouncy bass dictating the mellow groove, ably copied by the multi-tracked, punchy and very rhythmic vocals and reciprocal harmonies. The chorus is similar in style but sung in a smoother tone and it's good to hear the familiar bell of the ride and the lead guitar placed over a more funky, jittery groove. The words explore the connection between real musicianship – people playing their own instruments – and computer-based creativity: 'What about the sounds you steal'. It is suggested that there could be an opportunity to embrace both forms: 'There is no other way' and 'I think it's time to play'. It's an agreeable track that sits well amongst the various dynamics within the album.

'My Friend' (3.19) (I. Crichton, J. Gilmour)
It's Gilmour's turn to feature on a song written by both him and Ian Crichton, who also co-mixed this, as he did with track one. It's Crichton who starts the song, with a warm and mellow acoustic guitar deftly strummed and picked. Gilmour selects the clarinet as his preferred instrument to accompany his musical partner and this forms the basis of the song; the haunting melody continues throughout and it sounds fantastic. More synth and percussive flourishes are added throughout to this mild and peaceful number, where drums are not required. The strumming increases during the choruses, which also have an additional vocal added for increased spirit. Gilmour sings 'the

winter now is finally passed, I'm reacquainted with my dreams' and in the final chorus, 'Darkness falls on behind me, I'm starting now to find my way'. So the hard times are over and there is hope for the friend in the future. A pleasing song, its highlights being the interaction between the guitar and the clarinet and the vocal arrangement.

'Trust' (5.44) (Saga)
Sadler named this as one of his favourite tracks in the 2021 reissue liner notes, enthusing about its 'killer intro and great chord progressions'. The intro is impressive, with swelling and building synth patterns – think *'Jump'* by Van Halen – before you hear the first vocal, a loud, commanding 'Trust', with the next lines being 'you'll find it hard not to give it out' and so it progresses. You are left in no doubt about the track title, as the title is chanted 19 times by Gilmour as part of the verses and 22 times by Sadler in different parts of the chorus. This is a formidable track with some fantastic elements, in particular the smart arrangements of verse, chorus and bridge that create the changing dynamics between the three vocal sections, further strengthening the call and response element that propels the track. The instrumental section goes off the scale in terms of ability and dexterity. Jim Crichton and Doerner's rhythm section cement the foundations, allowing Gilmour and Crichton to go crazy with synth and guitar melodrama. It's a joyous section in a super song and one of the best parts of the album.

'It's Your Life' (4.10) (Saga)
There's a hint of 'Saga by numbers' to the beginning of the track and that's good. Sadler sings majestically during the moderately-paced verses, which tackle self-determination and the importance of personal responsibility. It is an upbeat, motivational message about owning your decisions and the subsequent benefits. The song has a tried and tested structure of chorus, verse, bridge, middle eight with a short guitar solo before a repeat-to-fade ending, with a few astute word changes along the way. Described as 'A catchy, symphonic prog piece' by *Sea Of Tranquillity*, it's well sung and played, with some delightful drumming and was released as a single, along with 'Trust' and 'That's As Far As I'll Go'.

'Footsteps In The Hall' (3.25) (Saga)
I've been looking forward to this. It's rare that you fall in love with a track on first hearing and I can only think of a few during my 50 years plus of seriously listening to music, including songs by Max Webster, Be Bop Deluxe, Blue Öyster Cult, The Tubes, Enchant and The Tiles. There are others, but none more so than Saga and this is another one. It's not easy to describe what it is exactly, but 'Footsteps In The Hall' has the lot in abundance. It's an awesome song, instantly appealing from the introductory keyboard hook, that's lively and uplifting, to Sadler's smooth, velvety and precise articulation

of the words. The melody is terrific and so is the earworm chorus: 'Do what you want to, you're too late I'm watching you'. Explosive stabs and alternating synth patterns form the interlude through the verse, then it's a glorious synthesiser solo and explosive fireworks from Ian Crichton. Those are amazing, but just as worthy is Jim Crichton's work 'behind the scenes', his phenomenal bass runs underpinning everything. It's great to revisit the original keyboard hook and the chorus ends the song all too soon. Lyrically, there is a haunting theme – 'wondering what are those footsteps in the hall' – and more than a nod to 'Leave Her Alone' from *Generation 13* in its soundscapes, theme and lyrical narrative – I play this track a lot. The band clearly felt the same and thankfully elected to choose it for *Symmetry*.

'Ice In The Rain' (5.01) (Saga)
The first verse of 16 seconds is smooth, with short, phrased vocals over a strummed guitar and colourful keyboard runs. The bridge turns up the intensity a notch and is catchy enough to feel more like a chorus. It's the same again on repeat with new lyrics and more musical changes, such as the initial break consisting of just vocals, synthesiser pads, excellent solos and the kick drum building to cue in the guitar solo. There's a fantastic bass groove underpinning the track, almost a solo in its own right and one of the best features of the song. The bridge and the instrumental section are also splendid, featuring delightful solos from Gilmour and then Crichton and Doerner is pretty good, too, with the solid beats and masterful fills.

'You Were Right' (4.05) (Saga)
A swifter pace is adopted here for this song. The verses consist of two short lines, prefixed by a two-word chant, always ending in 'it'. The bridge is just 'How do you feel, when you know that it's not real'. The chorus – 'Time to tell you, I believe you, now I know you were right' – indicates that this is about regret after ignoring someone's warning and realising it's too late. This is all sung with emotional purity and a broad tonal range, with the harmonies adding even greater impact. Musically, it's another great Saga offering that generally maintains an energetic speed of 160 bpm – quick but not quite in the realms of hardcore and thrash. There are lashings of heavy riffs and piano arpeggios, as well as a thundering rhythm section to propel the track. At 2.19, there's some great instrumental teamwork between Gilmour and Ian Crichton, with another superior demonstration of unity between the two. The track was quite rightly chosen for *Symmetry*, even if in abbreviated form.

'On The Other Side' (4.56) (Saga)
This would have made a great single; even though it's just short of five minutes long, it doesn't feel like that. It's a fabulous song – it's one of Sadler's favourites, which is probably why it reappears some 15 years later on *Symmetry*. Sadler enthused in the 2021 reissue liner notes that 'I've always

been a sucker for a good 3/4.' It is masterfully written and played and this time signature is almost disguised, but it is satisfying to count the waltz tempo. The number is made up of just three verses and an effortlessly addictive chorus. It starts with one of their longest and most majestic intros at 1.10, showcasing a plethora of complex polyrhythms and shifting synth and guitar patterns. The gentle arrangement and keyboard subtleties sound as though Gilmour has influenced much of this number and we are even treated to his accordion. The lyrics are hard to decipher: 'Just imagine what you can do on the other side'. My interpretation is a longing for something better and believing there's a different life waiting 'On The Other Side'. Overall, it's another great track that brings a wonderful album to an end

10,000 Days (2007)

Personnel:
Michael Sadler: vocals, keyboards
Jim Crichton: bass, keyboards
Jim Gilmour: keyboards, vocals
Ian Crichton: guitars
Brian Doerner: drums
Recorded and engineered by Saga
Drums recorded and engineered by Mark Fortuna
Produced by Saga
Mixed by Jim Crichton
Illustrations by Warren Flanagan
Graphic design by Patrick Zahorodniuk
Running time: 51:00
Release date: 19 October 2007
Label: Inside Out
Highest chart places: DE: 78, CN: did not chart, US: did not chart, UK: did not chart

In January 2007, Michael Sadler announced that he was leaving the band and this would be his last album with Saga. The message on his own and the band's website explained:

> After lengthy consideration and a healthy amount of soul searching, Michael has decided to announce his departure from Saga at the end of the year. Michael would also like to make it clear to everyone that his decision to leave is mostly of a personal nature! As far as the rest of the band are concerned, they have decided, for the moment, to keep all possible options open.

No one saw this coming except those closest to him. His open letter on 13 June 2007 is impeccably detailed in Ammerlaan's *Saga The Biography*, along with the details of a subsequent interview, in which Sadler explains that he needed to shift focus from the band and everything associated with it to spend more time with his family.

Following the release of *10,000 Days*, Saga went back on the road, selling out the vast majority of venues. Chris Sutherland (Kim Mitchell) temporarily filled in for Doerner, who was recovering from a heart attack. Sadler played his last show in Puerto Rico on 9 December 2007. The rest of the band began to audition for a new vocalist in March the following year.

10,000 days equate to 27 years and just over four months, the amount of time Sadler had been in Saga. It was therefore important to all concerned that Sadler's last album would be as good as it possibly could be to ensure it would be a fitting tribute and a legacy to a terrific singer, songwriter, musician and frontman. The album was released on CD in stylish digipack with an inspired space-themed cover, but as yet, no vinyl version exists.

'Lifeline' (5.36) (Saga)
'Lifeline' has the familiar traditional structure of other Saga songs (verse/chorus/bridge). The track has an emotive multi-synth opening that gradually speeds up to unveil a riffing guitar supported by layered synth instrumentation. The production is loud, balanced and organic, giving the bass and drums a real depth. The vocals are also well placed so that Sadler is bright and clear, bending the phrases in his usual fine style. So far, so good. At 2.40, the middle eight consists of soft synth lines over a funky groove – with the all-too-familiar 16th note hi-hat patterns – which then transitions into a solo section of two halves. Up first is Ian Crichton, then Gilmour, before they unite to augment each other superbly.

'Book Of Lies' (5.44) (Saga)
The inspiration for this song concerns tour itineraries and a lack of consultation and communication. You can sense the frustration in the second line of the first verse: 'It sounds a lot like showtime, but why am I up at six, no one told me we'd be playin' at Fort Dix' (a military base in Philadelphia). The music and Sadler's vocal delivery match their disdain; it's short and snappy, reflecting the band's annoyance and Doerner seems to be taking it out on his kit, this being his most explosive track, with a formidable, controlled frenzy across the toms. The track is long but is brimming with brilliantly constructed instrumentation and the guitar lead glides across the song's instrumental versions of the verse and chorus melody for 1:42, showcasing a good deal of Crichton's impressive repertoire. It's also a great live track, as witnessed on *Contact Live In Munich*, where Sadler milks the chorus in particular – 'Round and round it never stops, each day a new surprise' – sung to the audience, who are very happy to participate.

'Sideways' (4.53) (Saga)
Ian Crichton and Jim Gilmour duet intricately for 28 seconds before Doerner's fill signals the song's main melody, which is that of the chorus. Vocally, the verse has an effects-loaded, multi-tracked approach with smooth, elongated phrasing. It's a song with few words and as such, it's tricky to get to the nub of the meaning or the inspiration, but it seems to encourage looking at life and situations in different ways in order to 'grow'. The track has a mid-tempo pop-rock feel, paced at 131 bpm and there are some charming keyboard passages, but the best bit of the song is the instrumental section starting at 2.46, which has a wonderfully mysterious bass texture – it's hard to tell if this is guitar, Moog, or a combination, but I'd say Moog – that is splendid. The rest of the band lock in, bouncing along with the groove. It's a tender slice of

prog rock, with its technical virtuosity and intricate arrangements. It's highly inventive and very palatable.

'Can't You See Me Now?' (6.12) (Saga)
This is another six-minute-plus song and even though there are only nine tracks on *10,000 Days,* you do get your money's worth. Lyrically, it's not too challenging to follow or indeed write, it would seem. Every other line in the verses is 'Can't you see me now', or 'Don't you see me now', used on 14 occasions and nine other times during the bridge and choruses. It's written in the first person and has a ghostly quality, with its lingering melodies and invisibility notion, or it might just be a game of hide and seek. Gilmour and Ian Crichton start with potent, punchy synth-waves that sound immense, the Gilmour creating a simple but irresistible lick that travels through the verses. The vocals are more restrained, but are multi-tracked and harmonised at the end of lines, with the chorus being the most dynamic and poignant. At just over the halfway point, the instrumental segment kicks in and it's a monster. Several classic Saga-esque passages, featuring bombastic keyboards and intricate guitar phrases, are woven together magnificently to yield another prog musical masterpiece. One minute and 18 seconds later, it's the fourth verse, followed by the fourth bridge and final choruses to escort us to the end. Awesome.

'Corkentellis' (7.11) (Saga)
The longest track on the album is an instrumental. Saga don't do many instrumentals and why would they when they have such a gifted vocalist? This track was inspired by their three former managers, Corcoran, Kent and Ellis – hence the made-up word as the title. I imagine it was too challenging to write a set of words to sum up the band's feelings at the time, so they committed their multitude of emotions to a music-only piece. And it's an absolute barnstormer, teeming with jaw-dropping virtuosic displays from everyone. Sadler, Jim Crichton and Gilmour are credited with keyboards on the album sleeve, but on the *Spin It Again! Live In Munich* DVD, Sadler takes a rest, leaving the remaining four to perform the song. Mike Thorne replaced Doerner on this live set and is phenomenal, as are Crichton and Gilmour, showcasing incredibly fast fingers. On this studio version, there are similarly brilliant performances from all and it's fabulous to hear Doerner giving it a real go with some massive fills and Jim Crichton coming to the fore with his magnificent bass flair.

'More Than I Deserve' (5.22) (Saga)
The ballad and love song of the album – the words are earnest and sincere and beautifully sung and as such it's a track that would sit very comfortably on Sadler's solo album, *Clear,* released three years earlier, another worthy addition to a Saga fan's collection and appreciators of more emotive tunes.

Even though it's a gentler number, the composition is in familiar territory with the three vocal segments. My favourite line comes from the verse – 'More than I deserve and memories that we've burned remain, locked in yesterday' – as it describes a feeling of guilt about losing something good and trying to leave the painful memories behind. The first round of lyrics is completed by 2.12, with just Sadler, a synthesiser and a soft heartbeat in the distance. The leisurely pace resumes with a delightful lead guitar and tender cross-sticking, which graduates towards a full snare tap maintaining the pulse during the revisited chorus, which is captivating and thus repeated several times during the extended outro.

'Sound Advice' (5.17) (Saga)

The fade-out ending of the previous track perfectly sets up this edgy and upbeat number, featuring a cheeky guitar lick to open the proceedings. It's an engaging track that takes me back to 'Footsteps In The Hall' in its style and delivery, particularly the vocal melody. The verse has an odd time signature of 7/8 with some common time 4/4 phrasing – think 'Turn It On Again' by *Genesis* (13/8) – and it works superbly, especially with a brilliantly simple bass cajoling the song along. It's also compelling vocally, with dreamy harmonies in the spectacularly catchy chorus and as Saga occasionally do within the lyrics, they've harked back to song titles from the past; this time, it's 'The Ice Was Nice' (*Saga*). It's hairs on the back of your neck time when Sadler hits the notes on 'Part of the Plan' before Gilmour and Crichton take turns soloing in the instrumental section. At 4.17, it's back to the guitar intro and a run through of instrumental versions of the verse and chorus to the end. It's a splendid song that would be awesome live.

'10,000 Days' (4.31) (Saga)

I carefully scanned the lyrics of the album's title track to see if I could relate them in any way to the cover artwork, which shows astronauts and what looks like a very large shoe. According to the *Saga Germany* website, it 'features a large, metallic, insect-like head partially buried in a barren, reddish landscape.' A realistic interpretation would be that this is a clever symbolic image about scale, time and the impact of a long journey, which is now coming to an end. The booklet cover also has a footprint and an image of Saga from the early 1980s, so that would also fit in with the time theme. Likewise, the track has a reflective and melancholic tone both lyrically and musically, marking Sadler's 10,000 days with the band. The track recounts some of their experiences: 'So many faces now that we've seen 10,000 days and so many places', continuing with, 'We've been around the world, from East Lynn to LA'. It's a meaningful and expressive song with a simple structure, minimal soloing and a moderate pace in 6/8, with a gorgeous chorus and delightful piano refrains, making it an easy-flowing, pleasant and likeable track. It appears as a great live version on *Contact Live In Munich*.

'It Never Ends' (6.10) (Saga)
The last track on the album and what was thought to be Sadler's last ever track with Saga. The music has some typical Saga elements, featuring a more urgent tempo at 145 bpm. There are synth arpeggiated transitions throughout the first 20 seconds that also underpin the verse, hard riffing throughout when the vocals are absent, driving bass runs during the verses, a variety of guitar passages intersecting the verses and choruses and rich, polished vocals and harmonies during the bridge. So, it's everything you'd want from a Saga song. For the solo section, Gilmour delivers one of his most supreme synthesiser leads on the album, followed by another of Crichton's spontaneous guitar assaults. The ending is a bit disappointing, with another multi-chorus fade when a more innovative conclusion is desired for Sadler's final hurrah. And, as the bridge candidly proclaims, 'One door closes, one more opens, you won't know where or when, time to start again'. How true, but for now...

The Human Condition (2009)

Personnel:
Rob Moratti: vocals
Jim Gilmour: keyboards, vocals
Brian Doerner: drums
Ian Crichton: guitars
Jim Crichton: bass, keyboards
All songs written by Jim Gilmour, Jim Crichton, Ian Crichton, Rob Moratti
Guitars recorded at Dangling Carrot
All vocals recorded and engineered by Rob Moratti at Genuine Sound Studios
Drums recorded at Metalworks Studios
Produced by Saga
Engineer: Chris Crerar
Assistant engineer: Larry Curry
Mixed by Pat Regan at Sound Image Studios, Van Nuys, California
Illustrations by Balázs Pápay
Running time 47:16
Release date: 27 March 2009 (Europe) and 6 April 2009 (US, Canada)
Label: Inside Out
Highest chart places: DE: 91, CN: did not chart, US: did not chart, UK: did not chart

A new Saga and the first album without founder Michael Sadler. The band were never in doubt that they could and would continue; they just needed an able frontman who could not only convincingly deliver Saga's wide, varied and challenging portfolio, but could propel them into new territories, building on what they'd already achieved. This was a daunting task, but I'm happy to report that Rob Moratti (Final Frontier), who was chosen because he sang the best versions of 'On The Loose' and 'Wind Him Up' during auditions, did a tremendous job. He has an excellent voice, can write an interesting set of words and has contributed to a fabulous album that sits in high regard, lining up admirably amongst its peers. *The Human Condition* was well received, with Moratti being praised for his contribution to his only studio album with Saga. The band began working on the follow-up album with Moratti before Sadler contacted them during the mid-recording of *20/20* in 2012 to declare his wish to return. Ian Crichton reflected in *Prog* magazine in 2014:

> That was fun; Mike was gone and the pressure was on. It's still one of my favourite records in a way and it sold more than our previous record with Michael. Rob was a really nice guy, but he didn't have a lot of live experience and we were throwing him in front of a headline audience. Audiences had started to dwindle and the news was that, following the next record, financially, we wouldn't be able to tour. Sadler's call was, therefore, excellent timing.

The album was released on CD only, but it has a great digipack and is very similar in style and design to *10,000 Days*. Thankfully, there is a second Saga album featuring Moratti, *Heads Or Tails Live,* where you can hear him in full voice, belting out songs from that album. Like many fans, I'm grateful to him for briefly carrying the Saga torch, with two great albums. I play *The Human Condition* a lot.

'The Human Condition' (6.51) (J. Gilmour, J. Crichton, I. Crichton, R. Moratti)
Despite having a new frontman, the album begins with an instrumental, although technically, it does have a chorus: 'Running from the Human Condition'. Moratti's vocals are heavily masked with effects, meaning that it is hard to gauge the quality of his voice just yet – the tease is that we have to wait another seven minutes to form an initial opinion. This track has a slow, atmospheric opening formed of a synthesiser and a gentle, distant beat, then the main tempo arrives at a casual jogging pace. The production has an analogue warmth, with a lush top, middle and bottom, all penetrating impressively, the bass in particular being exquisitely lavish. There are masterful riffs by Gilmour and Crichton throughout and the intricate polyrhythmic patterns are a joy. This is an exceptional number from a reinvigorated Saga, with extensive, rapid soloing and solid grooving.

'Step Inside' (4.56) (J. Gilmour, J. Crichton, I. Crichton, R. Moratti)
Saga had three lyricists previously and generally, it wasn't too difficult to identify who wrote what when Saga were credited with the whole song. Usually, Gilmour sang his own songs, often based on introspective themes and emotional resonance. Sadler wrote in a similar style, whereas Jim Crichton was the innovator and storyteller. Where does Moratti sit? 'Step Inside' is more in line with Sadler, being conversational, advisory and linear. The structure is as Sadler would present it, too, although the verses are incredibly short and the bridge is even shorter, with just 'Step Inside' sung, so it's the chorus with the majority of words. Moratti's voice is worlds apart from Sadler's – he's not as soulful, theatrical, or choral, but I'd say more rock-infused, with an expressive, controlled vibrato and precise articulation. He's definitely suited to Saga and it's obvious why they chose him. At 33 seconds in, Moratti belts out his first lines, the mini verse and it sounds splendid. He certainly hangs on to the last note much longer than his predecessor and bends the notes more. Musically, it's Saga with a twist, with plenty of dynamic changes, fluid soloing and complementary instrumentation. It's a decent enough track, but you get the impression they are warming up and there's better to come.

'Hands Of Time' (5.29) (J. Gilmour, J. Crichton, I. Crichton, R. Moratti)
It appears that more thought has been given to these lyrics and Saga's mild obsession with 'time' has inspired Moratti to lift it from the past for this

number, which also has a hint of the 'Chapters' saga. The lyrics in the chorus are effective, referencing the unstoppable flow of time and the inevitability of change: 'Through the narrow hands of time, an open door will lead you far and wide'. The rest of the band supplement this poetry superbly, starting with spacious synths and a graceful melody that allows Moratti to drift to a lower range. At 2.10, the meter gently increases with a sympathetic backbeat and musical accompaniment. The song, however, does belong to Moratti, as he moves smoothly between vocal registers, the higher notes being spectacular. This would have been a great live track because of its delightful sing-along chorus.

'Avalon' (4.48) (J. Gilmour, J. Crichton, I. Crichton, R. Moratti)
Think back to ***Marathon*** and its title track, with the chorus, 'It takes time to get to Avalon, that's why we're on this Marathon'. It's probably not a coincidence that it's been resurrected, as Moratti's co-lyricist for this number is Jim Crichton. Careful analysis doesn't reveal any obvious links or sequels to that theme, but it does, however, contain some out-of-this-world (literally) stanzas, emerging from the realms of fantasy and the mystical. It's good old-fashioned prog, much of it nonsensical, but very descriptive and brilliant. There are too many such lines to quote, but it's fun to try to understand where Moratti is coming from and I can overlook some of the obvious rhymes as he continues where he left off from the previous track. The vocals are fabulous, making it easy to appreciate his dexterity and range across the verses and chorus, with Gilmour expertly singing the bridge. The first round of words is done in just over two minutes and then the lengthy instrumental segment meanders gracefully in between passages, with some magical moments from guitar and synth, great drum fills and mighty bass undercurrents, all thoroughly enjoyable. 'Trees floating upside down', 'a boat with a hole', 'a rat and a snake heading underground' and 'an egg stone'. What more could you want?

'A Number With A Name' (4.51) (J. Gilmour, J. Crichton, I. Crichton, R. Moratti)
Jim Crichton and Moratti collaborate once more to provide the lyrics and melody, but the lyrics are difficult to decipher. The verses include 'driving' metaphors, the chorus states that 'someone turned the lighthouse down and it began to rain', which doesn't seem to fit and the bridge is just the song's title, which makes it difficult to pin down the song's real meaning. Musically, however, everything seems to slot together perfectly, with the track being skilfully sung alongside many traditional Saga components. Doerner comes alive and throws in a couple of magnificent solos and Crichton and Gilmour likewise deliver solos of the expected high standard. The song has the same flow and similar melody to 'Footsteps In The Hall' (again), as the pair start with an impudent call and response, speaker to speaker. The vibe continues

during the track, with a catchy chorus, housing more intriguing and confusing words, over a mid-tempo pace. It's a competent performance by a motivated band and all in all, it's a very good song indeed.

'Now Is Now' (4.12) (J. Gilmour, J. Crichton, I. Crichton, R. Moratti)
This easy-going pop-oriented track is pleasant enough, but it doesn't really excel in any areas – the bar is pretty high on this album. The slower tempo of 100 bpm allows room and time for Moratti to demonstrate another side to his vocal aptitude, which is warm, heartfelt and self-reflective. The bulk of the song is the repeated lingering chorus, the verses being a minuscule two lines and the bridge is just 'Now Is Now', with Moratti effortlessly riding on the groove, hitting some impressively high notes. The music is given a mechanical feel due to the initial drum machine-like sound on the kit and the echoed effects. Much of the track is instrumental, consisting of crunching riffs, synth arpeggios sequences, bright lead guitar and creative drum and bass fills. It's a pleasant track that effectively showcases the new Saga.

'Let It Go' (4.47) (J. Gilmour, J. Crichton, I. Crichton, R. Moratti)
This is a fantastic song. Moratti is exceptional, arguably giving his best performance on the album, soaring up and down his range, with just enough vibrato, perfect dynamics and textured phrasing. His three-part harmonies on the chorus are goosebump-inducing. Ian Crichton also steps up to showcase more of his fluid, energetic, magnificent hooks, both heavy and melodic and his solos are stupendous. There are glimpses of Gilmour's keyboard and piano prowess hidden beneath vocals and guitar, but at 4.27, he all too briefly comes to the fore and it's terrific. Doerner's tempo is solid, producing arguably the best fills on the album and his kick drum's perfect placement is particularly noticeable, being high in the mix.

'Crown Of Thorns' (5.46) (J. Gilmour, J. Crichton, I. Crichton, R. Moratti)
There's no messing about as we're thrown in at the deep end with an intricate guitar intro, Ian Crichton's fingers moving at pace; it's a 'silent' count of four and everyone's in, even Moratti: 'Truth is Born, mystified, till the day it hunts you down, crown of thorns, dignified, fills my head without a sound'. The mind of Moratti is a mysterious place: the words appear, not necessarily in order, with some improbable terms, phrases and rhymes. For example, the chorus opens with 'The scattered profanity honored and written in stone'. This is a dark, self-reflective episode; the crown of thorns imagery suggests being forced into a role that may look honourable but is actually painful and carrying expectations, criticism, or pressure that others don't see. It makes interesting reading and follows similar patterns of ambiguity and personal interpretation that are very typical of Saga. Musically, we are treated to more exceptional performances, with Doerner showing off some impressive double kick drum patterns in the bridge and extravagant brilliance from Ian Crichton

and Gilmour when it comes to their turn at 2.57 and towards the end of the track. The band's quality never diminishes and the mix and production quality raise the track way above the average.

'You Look Good To Me' (5.22) (J. Gilmour, J. Crichton, I. Crichton, R. Moratti)
The album has been extremely satisfying thus far. Having a new singer hasn't changed Saga's unique brand of prog rock; it's just been given a new flavour and it's tasty. This track has both Moratti and Jim Crichton with pens in hand, composing the lyrics. Plenty of words adorn the CD's booklet and they flow regally from Moratti, but again, effort is needed to decrypt them. The word 'Ladder' is used quite a bit, harking back to *Saga* and verse four ends with more referencing, such as 'Listen To Your Heart' from *Behaviour*. The song has a comfortable groove at 155 bpm with a swing feel and it starts with crunchy, staccato guitar riffs, joined by Doerner playing his kit with great fluency – they sound amazing. Jim Crichton's smooth and meticulous technique is tightly aligned with Doerner's bass drum. The vocal melody is enduring and Moratti's articulation is precise right across the range, even when extending notes at the end of the lines. At 3.03, the dynamics intensify for the instrumental section, as good as anything from the previous eight tracks. It has an energetic, jerky, almost unsettling groove, but Gilmour and Crichton pay no heed and endeavour to produce smooth, sophisticated breaks and solos. It sounds good to me. Great track, tremendous album.

20/20 (2012)

Personnel:
Michael Sadler: lead vocals, keyboards
Jim Gilmour: main keyboards, vocals
Ian Crichton: guitar
Jim Crichton: bass and keyboards
Brian Doerner: drums
All songs written by Saga
Recorded at Massive Studios-Los Angeles, Stan Portley Studios, Dangling Carrot Studios, Sparta Studios and Good Sheppard Studios
Engineered by Pat Regan, Mark Fortuna, Ian Crichton, Jim Crichton and Jim Gilmour
Mixed at Massive Studio, Los Angeles, California
Mixing engineer: Pat Regan
Front cover concept by Dean Meehan
Design by Alexander Mertsch
Band cover by Darko
DVD concept, filming and editing by Mike Filsinger
Running time: 48:16
Release date: 6 July 2012
Label: earMusic
Highest chart places: DE: 13, CN: did not chart, US: did not chart, UK: did not chart

Michael Sadler is back in the band and ready to record and tour again with Saga, the band he helped to create. He felt that he had made the right decision to leave, but equally it was the right decision to return, the latter reinforced by the fans' positive reaction on the subsequent tour. The songs were written during Rob Moretti's tenure, so Sadler stepped in to add his own ideas and vocal flavouring. On the CD's bonus DVD, he commented that he was pleased with the 'very good' album and enthused that they were ready to take it on the road.

Sadler and Jim Crichton came up with *20/20* as the title based on it being their 20th studio album and a reference to 20/20 vision following Jim Gilmour's successful operation for a detached retina that occurred during the previous tour.

The album received a reasonable reception in North America, even though it did not chart there, but once again, it was Germany who mostly embraced the band and their new release, helping it to reach number 13 on their charts.

The special edition digipack CD contains a bonus DVD, *Behind The Scenes Documentary*, of Saga's fall tour rehearsals, which provides further details of the Sadler's return, as does the following press release:

> Eagle Rock Entertainment/earMusic (Saga's new label) are proud to announce the Canadian release of *20/20*, the 20th studio album from Canadian

> progressive rock icons Saga. Finally reunited again with their original singer, Michael Sadler, *20/20* is the ultimate AOR/progressive rock album. *20/20* will be released in the US on 28 August. Their musical style is defined by prominent guitar riffs, often in harmony with a synthesiser and complex keyboard arrangements. The album features ten brand new songs, never missing the distinctive sound of Saga's legendary hits. With striking keyboard sounds and Michael Sadler's stunning vocals, the album has all that it takes to become an instant fan favourite as well as a worldwide hit.

This article also refers to Gilmour's recent eye operation that gave him 20/20 vision. Martin Popoff's interview with Michael Sadler, in July 2012, also provided some interesting insights. 'How does it relate to recent Saga albums?' Popoff asked. Sadler responded:

> It's weird because I was brought in, not at the 11th hour, but when it was decided I was coming back, they had already written 95% of the music, so I was handed essentially a finished product, which is weird for me because I was always involved with the songwriting in the past. So it was a whole new ballgame for me. It sounds like vintage Saga; I think there are the elements of what got people excited about the band in the beginning.

Three separate recording studios were used and although it doesn't say so on the sleeve notes, it's likely that Saga themselves produced it. The album was reissued in 2014 by earMusic as a limited-edition red vinyl version, but with no bonuses.

It's been two years since Saga's last long player and five years since Sadler's last album with the band. I suspect that fans will be pleased and intrigued in equal measures, so what's it like? Production-wise, it's polished and precise, superbly showcasing the arrangements, songwriting and performing talent on show.

'Six Feet Under' (4.56) (Saga)

'Six Feet Under' is a great example of the production values and the newfound enthusiasm of the return of Sadler. It's a formidable opener. Gilmour is up first with some dramatic synth stabs before Sadler joins in with those familiar dulcet tones, multi-tracked, but infectious and in less than 20 seconds into the track, we're comforted. He sounds magnificent and has lost none of his range, technique and unique skills in creating and delivering melodies. The track's structure doesn't follow a usual blueprint. The first verse is followed by a fairly lengthy instrumental section before the bridge, which does adhere to customary Saga – a call and response approach, with Sadler on the 'response'. The call is a joint affair that lyrically increases by 'two feet' on each line, ending at 'twelve feet'. Doerner, too, has brought his 'A' game with some super-fast drum rolls and aggressive double-time beats just after the first chorus. The anticipated solo section comes in at 3.49 and Ian Crichton's special abilities are evidenced early on in the album. It's a sprightly track of many light and shade moments, commanding vocals, particularly in the chorus, setting high expectations for the rest of the album. It's one of three tracks from *20/20* that appear on the *Spin It Again* live DVD.

'Anywhere You Wanna Go' (5.29) (Saga)
Eagle Rock's PR machine claimed that the 'catchy, high-energy 'Anywhere You Wanna Go' clarifies that Saga's original trademark sound is still going strong' – it's true. Lyrically, it's possibly advocating a sense of freedom and opportunity. It's an absorbing, habitual Saga with Gilmour providing the lead melody for Ian Crichton to chug against, with the roles reversing later on. Jim Crichton and Doerner ably hold things together at the slower pace of 103 bpm. Saga don't often have a dead stop mid song, but at 2.19, a silent count of four brings in short and neat Crichton's solo. There's more from him towards the end, duetting with Gilmour and possibly Sadler, who's also credited with keyboards. The live rendition on *Spin It Again* is just as good.

'Ellery' (4.08) (Saga)
Could this be the return of Ellery Sneed, the perfectionist who appeared and disappeared all within the space of 5:43 on Saga's debut album? A perusal of the lyrics doesn't indicate so, but if you're playing Saga 'bingo', there's at least 'worlds apart'. 'Ellery' is a chorus-heavy track with Sadler echoing the main lines and phrases during the bridge. Although this technique works, for me, it's a bit overdone on this track and I'd be more content with the music itself having that space and being allowed more breathing room. It is, however, one of the album's more introspective and heartfelt songs on the album, with a delicate tone and atmospheric arrangements, established by Gilmour's floating synth refrain. More evidence that Saga can write compelling and melodic pieces. Key moments enhanced by the tasteful production are the gorgeous harmonies, the gentle 6/8 waltz-like pulse, the brief, subtle tempo changes and Doerner demonstrating his individuality in feel and expression. I'm sure the melody from 'Time To Go', from *Silent Knight,* is in there.

'Spin It Again' (4.41) (Saga)
This track reminds me of It Bites, the excellent UK band who were similar to Saga in their songwriting ability and musicianship, with its crisp opening guitar riff, soft synth padding and pop leanings. Gilmour begins by lulling us into a false sense of security with some delicate synth padding before Crichton bursts in with one of his signature infectious riffs and it's nice and heavy, right up there in the mix – a headbangers paradise. For more of the same, check out any of Ian Crichton's solo releases. There's slightly more mellow strumming when Sadler nudges in the first verse, which is smooth and expressive. The theme could be about rediscovery and renewal, perhaps

regarding Sadler's return, or it might just be about playing records: 'Spin it again, take a little from the middle, let it ride on the inside and spin it again, one more time'. Doerner's tom rolls are magnificent and as for Crichton's solo at 3.07, it's a trip through a harmonic landscape, creative and breathtaking. The faders are up high to make sure we don't miss anything in the mix and not surprisingly, this beast appears on the *Spin It Again* live release.

'Another Day Out Of Sight' (4.18) (Saga)
It's Jim Gilmour's turn for lead vocals and he may well be the lyricist, too, on this track about emotionally drifting through life or a relationship. It's an orthodox Gilmour song to suit his range and timbre, seeping with vulnerability. It's a ballad but with an odd, syncopated rhythmic pattern for the verse. The instrumental section at three minutes isn't conventional Saga either, with Doerner preferring the toms and a simple bass drum/snare pattern, as Crichton makes full use of his whammy bar and pedals, it appears, during his solo. It's these elements that lift the number and provide Gilmour the momentum to deliver a charming song.

'One Of These Days' (4.46) (Saga)
Another track with a substantial number of words that take up one and a half sides of the CD's booklet and almost a full column on the vinyl version. Of course, many are repeated, but it's still a lot. Sadler is back behind the mic to render them, which he does with confidence and ease, his chosen melodies all being immediately appealing. There's an upbeat, almost joyful feel to the song and the words also have positivity at their core: 'One of these days you're gonna shake those chains that bind you'. The tempo remains at 141 bpm for most of the track, but dips and varies just before the midway point to allow for an 'improvised' instrumental assault before things resume. All are on great form: Sadler shines, Gilmour's piano flourishes add extra value and Jim Crichton is solid and inventive across the disparate sections. One of the highlights comes at 4.09 when you are just preparing for a chorus ad infinitum, ending instead with a controlled yet monstrous 'thrash bang' – a masterclass in musical tension.

'Ball And Chain' (4.17) (Saga)
Continuing the chain motif referred to in the previous track's first verse – 'One of these days your gonna shake those chains that bind you' – this song's chorus continues: 'We think it's more than a little strange that you've found a name for that ball and chain'. The theme appears to be about being emotionally tied to something that limits your freedom, even though you know it's holding you back, which dictates the track's brooding and melancholic mood. At 2.40, there's a twist into the middle eight, which features a sensational yet all-too-short 32-second piano solo from Gilmour, one of the highlights of the whole album. The song is accentuated by a

stabbing, jerky rhythm beneath the vocals and some nice harmonies – all in all, its a splendid arrangement and presentation. The concluding bridge proclaims, 'You know we're all the same, but sometimes rules get broken'. Indeed.

'Lost For Words' (4.34) (Saga)
This is Sadler at his evocative best. His personality shines through and his singing on this song is magnificent; when he hits the notes on the third line of the chorus, 'and somebody gave me', prepare for the tingling. It's a power ballad and an exceptionally good one, with a graceful acoustic guitar, soothing synth padding and gentle crooning in the first verse: 'When the dust had settled near and the sky had all but cleared, enough to view my destination'. The vocal energy increases in the chorus, starting with 'Somebody saved me' and including the emotional notes hit on the third line. A steady groove enters for the second verse and continues for most of the song. There's no overplaying at any time, the band providing the bedrock for Sadler to excel. Other notable moments are the simple but instantly recognisable Gilmour piano interlude, a piece that's wholesome and mellow. Ian Crichton conjures up a heartfelt lead and Doerner, too, has his moments, with some acutely placed independent snare and bass drum phrasing mirroring Jim Crichton's sublime runs. It's an introspective and reflective lyric and a marvellous song.

'Show And Tell' (4.42) (Saga)
Contrasting from the previous track, 'Show And Tell' has Saga in a more exuberant mood, with a quirky guitar melody line and a punchy ostinato rhythm at a moderate strutting pace. It's also an interesting track because the first line of the verses are harmonised by Sadler and Gilmour, but the words are extended and sustained, almost slurred, whilst Sadler goes it alone for the next line. Appealing, too, is a short guitar break that starts at the bridge, then roams from section to section, even across the vocal passages, without detracting from them. At 2.32, we're interrupted by a thudding bass drum, a piano breakdown, a lively guitar break, then an exquisite synthesiser solo before Gilmour hands back to Ian Crichton and his lead guitar. This is monumental, lasting almost 60 seconds before it's replaced by the first iterations of the song. It's that quirky guitar line that's the last thing we hear.

'Till The Well Runs Dry' (6.20) (Saga)
The album's closer is an epic that consists of six quite lengthy verses, four catchy choruses and one of Crichton's best ever guitar solos. It starts with a slow build, with Sadler almost talking the first two verses with minimum accompaniment, just Gilmour's synth melodies and Crichton strumming, before Doerner and the rest of the band transport him through the next two verses to 1.49, the first chorus. Here, Sadler increases the intensity, chanting

out a melodious offering with some excellent lyrics: 'Run to the well, until the well runs dry, or my thirst is finally satisfied, shake that tree until the bough breaks free, get myself a good look inside'. The words are introspective; my best interpretation would be about persistence and determination to give everything you have until the very end. Note, too, the previous Saga song title references (again). Before verse five, there's a short, haunting guitar refrain, complete with echoey effects, leading to another verse and chorus before the instrumental and that solo. I've avoided the word 'blistering' until now. I can't think of a better one – it's simply awesome, with the shredding element being my favourite. Underneath this is an exquisite bassline and his runs on this section in particular are inspired. Overall, it's another excellent album closer. Welcome back, Michael Sadler.

Sagacity (2014)

Personnel:
Michael Sadler: lead vocals, keyboards
Ian Crichton: guitar
Jim Crichton: bass, keyboards
Jim Gilmour: main keyboards, vocals
Mike Thorne: drums, vocals
All songs written by Saga
The recordings were created and mixed using 'PreSonus Studio One' software at various locations
Michael Sadler's vocals were recorded and engineered by Michael Vandeven, Vandeven Enterprises and by Tom Bettie, Attic Studios
Mixed and mastered by Brian Foraker
Front cover illustrations created by Bernt Kulseth
Design by Alexander Mertsch
Photography by Alexander Mertsch
Release date: 27 June 2014
Label: earMusic
Running time: 50:50
Highest chart position: DE: 17, CN: did not chart, US: did not chart, UK: did not chart

The band were interviewed by Rich Wilson for *Prog* (issue 48) in August 2014. Titled 'The Next Chapter', the feature opened with:

> The Oxford Dictionary defines a saga as 'a long story of heroic achievement'. Having survived disco, the 1980s, an ill-fated brush with popular TV and the departure of not one but two singers, melodic proggers Saga couldn't have foreseen how appropriate their name would be. Now they are back with the latest entry in their epic tale: new album *Sagacity*.

It's an interesting and insightful article looking back and forward, with a focus on the latest release. It explains that for this album, the band decamped to a secluded cottage on the shores of Canada's Lake Erie, having the freedom to be creative and promote individual ideas, without the perils of cabin fever. The album is thought to be a 'departure' from the last two releases, possessing contemporary and highly accessible songs that allude to their early works. Creating such an album was the result of a deliberate attempt to move away from the complexity and return to a more organic sound. Ian Crichton explained to *Prog* magazine in 2014:

> On this record, the only thing we talked about before we wrote a note was our first four records. Saga have always been about melodic prog rock. Our arrangements on the first few records had some magical parts that worked

well together, so we thought it would be great to write a record that sounded like those early albums. The music isn't too complicated and without us going crazy on wild licks. We didn't want 600 notes flying at you at once. I'm personally really tired of that. I remain optimistic that our latest album has the potential to revive Saga's fortunes. With regard to the name of the album, it was nothing too clever, it would appear; the band were just looking through a dictionary and came across it.

Sagacity was mixed using PreSonus Studio One software by Brian Foraker in Nashville, who mixed the album during Saga's 2014 European tour and used 'Source Live' internet streaming software to enable Jim Crichton to listen to the mixes live using a pair of studio monitors connected to his iPhone. His monitoring studio was set up in various hotels and dressing rooms across Europe. As long as there was a good internet connection, 'we were mixing!'

Brian Doerner had to leave the band due to health reasons, which was sad, but Mike Thorne brings a new dimension and impetus. This is Thornes' first studio album with Saga, recruited by having the best YouTube video audition. He stayed with the band and can be seen and heard on several live releases, including the recording that accompanies the CD version of *Sagacity,* a previously unreleased full live concert, *Saga Hits Live At Swri Rockarena 2013*.

This could well be Saga's last album of new material, so it's one to savour and treasure, with 12 songs totalling just over 50 minutes packed into the CD. The album notes provide a comprehensive account of the mixing process, but not the recording process, which is a shame, as it would be interesting, too. A double vinyl package is needed to cater to the generous musical offering, but it doesn't include the live recording.

'Let It Slide' (4.49) (Saga)
The album opens with a recognisable intro with plenty of atmosphere created by keyboard padding and gently controlled guitar feedback. It's not long before there's heavier riffing as a prelude to the first verse, which drops to a more modest tone. First observations are the distorted guitar, the standout bass groove and the strength of the vocals. This does feel like a different production than the last album, with lots of bottom end and an overall more grungy and raw sound, reminiscent of *Pleasure And The Pain*. Jim Crichton's presence is all over this track, which is a bonus, whilst brother Ian also excels on guitar with some amazing runs in an extended instrumental section defined by the twin and solo leads of Ian Crichton and Jim Gilmour. The song's structure is reassuringly familiar, if not particularly inventive, but there are interesting passages to maintain focus, with some wacky, playful guitar and more grounded, supportive synth patterns. The lyrics seem to explore themes of forgiveness, acceptance and letting go of grudges and negativity. A very good start to the album with an absorbing track, but it does need a few spins to fully appreciate its merits.

'Vital Signs' (3.27) (Saga)
Not to be confused with fellow Canadians Rush's track of the same name (*Moving Pictures,* 1981). This is pure Saga, although it's a shorter track and lacks an instrumental section or any soloing. The distorted guitar is further back in the mix and the first verse is quiet, with mainly Sadler and synth. The song progresses with a jittery rhythm created by syncopated bass drum accents and some other nifty drumming by Thorne. The bridge starts with 'We're barely human at the best of times' and ends the track with the line 'Best not forget to check your vital signs'. Body temperature, heart rate, breathing rate, blood pressure and oxygen in the blood. Checked and like this track, it's all good.

'It Doesn't Matter (Who You Are)' (3.59) (Saga)
Jim Gilmour has two lead vocal songs on the album and this is the first. It's a slow, humble tempo at a steady walking pace of 106 bpm. It does plod a tad and I think upping the tempo and maybe giving it more of a swing might make it more appealing. It still works, though, particularly with Gilmour's warm and balanced tenor range. He's dealing with the theme of valuing people for who they truly are, rather than judging them by labels, status, or appearances. He's added a more contemporary twist by bringing into focus social media: 'You can reach me on Facebook right now'. Vocally, standout elements include the line 'talk to me', sung with heaps of conviction and fortunately its reprised several times during the number. When the singing stops, at 1.49, Ian Crichton enters for one of his more eccentric and quirky leads, reaching for a more unusual note sequence than we're used to from him. It's a charming song providing a respite from the normal proceedings.

'Go With The Flow' (5.26) (Saga)
There's a great drum roll to cue in a lively chorus melody, governed by an enthusiastic guitar lick, before giving way to stylish acoustic flatpicking. Sadler then sings with much sincerity to a stripped-back arrangement of mainly acoustic guitar, a gentle drum pattern and soothing harmonies. The chorus, first in at 1.22, goes up a notch, still keeping the mood serene, the main difference from the verse being the guitar riffing and a more urgent groove. Gilmour plays a blinder at 2.33, with a bright, fresh synthesiser solo before Crichton's heavy strumming. At 4.29 and it's well worth the short wait for Crichton's lead, which is an astonishing display of fretwork. During the instrumental segments, Thorne and Jim Crichton are grooving the backbeat underneath with a series of staccato stabs and attacks that make it difficult to guess the time signature – I'm guessing 7/8 – it's phenomenal. It's also great to hear some double bass drumming towards the end.

'Press 9' (3.48) (Saga)
Gilmour's second lead vocal outing is for a really odd song. Odd as in peculiar and odd as in that it doesn't match anything on this album or

anything that Saga have ever done. The song explores the idea of pressing a number on the phone to get rid of one's troubles. It follows the same pattern throughout, such as 'if you want the IRS to go away, go ahead press 9' and so on. Different numbers resolve different issues: regretting telling a lie, being stuck in traffic, wanting to kill, an evil neighbour, a team about to lose, gaining weight, etc. 'Go ahead press' is harmonised to add a texture. There is a chorus, in which Sadler is prominent and it's sedate and soothing, ending with 'Cos now I'm right at home'. Thorne and Jim Crichton are nowhere to be seen (it would appear), as there is no rhythm section required, but there is a place for Ian and a seductive run through the chords on acoustic and an expressive solo. I wasn't keen on first hearing, but it does grow on you and should be taken as intended (I think) – not too seriously.

'Wake Up' (2.34) (Saga)
The shortest track on the album – it's unusual for a Saga number to be well under three minutes. It begins with a loud 'Wake Up' from Gilmour. Crichton breaks the slumber with a rollicking, heavy guitar hook that delivers – he's in his element. He exits for the verse, leaving both Jims to create an ethereal, haunting texture, with a cool walking bassline and resonant synth padding for Sadler to respond with a supreme breathy interpretation of the words. This is Saga in a more unusual frame, with a more experimental structure, but the musicianship is still outstanding. Jim Crichton is on fire on this track and Thorne is sublime, with cleverly placed independent ghost notes on snare and bass drum to further light up the track. The band have packed a lot into this condensed song with a plethora of dynamic swings, rhythmic variants and changing melodies.

'Don't Forget To Breathe' (3.24) (Saga)
Following on from *Marathon*'s 'Breathing Lessons', Ian Crichton is back with another gritty, distorted guitar hook, at about the same level in the mix as Sadler's voice for the chorus, which begins the tale. He cuts through a bit more during the shorter verses, which have a great melody and so does the bridge, where Crichton's hook follows Sadler's vocal melody. The track is paced at a mid-tempo stride, allowing Thorne to keep it relatively simple and Jim Crichton underpins the momentum with flair and fluidity, producing a constant, infectious rumble. The solo comes in at 2.01 and it's excellent as expected, ending with a charming twin lead. The title is mentioned just twice in the song, its meaning perhaps being about getting caught up in the grind and expectations of life, with a stark reminder to slow down and stay grounded. It's one of the best tracks on the album and would have made a successful single.

'The Further You Go' (4.04) (Saga)
Similar to other tracks on the album, the initial vocals are laid down without full band accompaniment, just a jangly guitar line and synth soundscape, later joined

by a solid rhythmic backbone of drums and bass. The groove moves between 4/4 and 3/4 time signatures, something Saga do occasionally, which keeps the arrangements fresh. Gilmour impresses with a marvellous synth solo and there's even a canon-style section, a structured approach where the lead voice begins the melody and the follower's voice imitates it after a short delay. Sadler and Gilmour sing this with beautifully smooth harmonies, more evidence of innovation and progression and pushing their own boundaries. This is a great track about ambition, chasing your dreams and making the most of life's journey.

'On My Way' (5.15) (Saga)
The first 1:15 is a gorgeous ambient synthesiser refrain underscored by atmospheric padding, hinting at a church setting. Thorne coaxes in the first verse with a short fill, sung in hushed, laid-back tones. Vocally, this is the feel throughout the song, with both Sadler and Gilmour working perfectly in tandem as Ian Crichton's guitar phrasing follows them very closely. The track has some striking melodies as it ebbs and flows. The tempo is a constant 124 bpm, so nicely accessible, driven by Jim Crichton's pulsing basslines. At the mid-section at 3.43, the pace increases dramatically up to an energetic, playful beat, enabling Crichton and Gilmour to flourish, the latter introducing superb piano trills; it's also worth noting Thorne's complex kick drum theatrics. The song is about recognising the time to change, and, of course, there have to be references to previous Saga releases: 'On my way, I know of a better place, don't be late, here comes our face-to-face and We've climbed the ladder'. It's a fabulous song worthy of repeat plays due to its indelible melodies and hooks.

'No Two Sides' (3.58) (Saga)
Of all the tracks on 'Sagacity', this is the one that feels more like album filler or a bonus track. It's a bit vanilla compared to the rest. It's agreeable and satisfying enough, but it just lacks dynamism and energy and yearns to be more innovative like 'Press 9' or 'On My Way'. A compelling, resonating guitar prelude leads into a familiar structure. The instrumental section starts at 3.14 and closes the track. It consists of a gentle synth piece, but there aren't any solos. The melodies throughout are pleasing enough, but the chorus is slightly disappointing and lacks conviction; however, the bridge is catchy: 'Two for the show, my oh my, how we have grown, two for the show, think of the seeds we have sown'. So, there is a positive message about changing situations and destinations, facing fears and finding something new. There are authoritative and competent performances from the band with some great touches, including the synth ostinato and the low-register vocals. Unfortunately, that's not enough to propel it to greater heights.

'Luck' (3.39) (Saga)
A promising start with a wonderful instrumental segment dominated by deep, resonating, chest-thumping bass notes, I'd say on a Moog. The power and

clarity evidenced here is a great example of the consummate recording, mixing and mastering of the album. There are more soundscapes courtesy of Gilmour and a terrific guitar hook courtesy of Crichton. This is halted suddenly by the verse, with minimal backing and a cross-stick backbeat laying down a slowish tempo. Gilmour sings the bridge, underscored by singular synth pads. The chorus is an incredibly well-arranged heavy metal monster, with both Sadler and Gilmour impeccably singing and supplying amazing harmonies. It's as good a chorus as any on the album and watch out particularly for the line 'celebrate your fate', which lands perfectly and is one of those goosebumps moments. There's at least one direct reference to luck, that being a 'Black Cat', but I'd say the song is rooted around the theme of how much of life comes down to chance and learning to accept, even embrace, whatever you're dealt. At 2.32, the penetrating lead guitar, over one of the slower segments, is fabulous. Sadler doesn't often repeat melodies from previous numbers, but when he belts out the lines 'Searching for something of a fortunate kind' and 'Just a little bit more', from the verse, you're transported back to 1983's 'The Intermission' on *Head Or Tails*, specifically the melody on the line 'I fall inside'. He was brilliant then and he still is.

'I'll Be' (6.21) (Saga)

The end of an era – it's the last track on Saga's final album of new and original material. It's track number 222 in their portfolio, depending on what you include and it's the longest track on this album by a minute. It's got a magnificent opening, with Ian Crichton displaying the depth and breadth of his ability, dexterity and genius for 1:07. Further confirmation, if it was needed, that he can play any genre. For this lengthy curtain raiser, he's chosen a phenomenal Spanish style, picking and strumming a polyrhythmic motif using multiple guitar parts, which reminded me of *The Security Of Illusion*. He immediately swaps back to the distorted heavy electric guitar sound, much favoured on the album, for the verse prelude, with Gilmour's sublime piano flourishes as a contrast, more classical than in the slow and solemn verse. Jim Crichton infiltrates the mix with magical bass themes and Thorne eases through many intricate drum patterns. The song has another exceptional chorus melody and lyrically, it's about commitment and reassurance, promising to be there for someone no matter what changes or uncertainties come. The break at 3.50 features Ian Crichton lavishly shredding during a clean, soulful breakdown. The song appears to finish at 5.36, but no, it proceeds with the distant sound of church bells, then four singular strikes to end. A fitting finale to a classy album.

Symmetry (2021)

Personnel:
Michael Sadler: vocals
Jim Crichton: bass
Ian Crichton: guitars, mandolin, banjo
Jim Gilmour: clarinet, accordion, piano, vocals
Mike Thorne: kick, snare, kitchen percussion
Additional musicians:
Shane Cook: fiddle
Stephany Seki: cello
Beth Silver: cello
Seren Sadler: guest vocalist
Recorded at Goodnight Nashville, Cliffhanger Studio, Symphony Court Studios
Cellos recorded at Desolation Studios, Toronto, Dangling Carrot Studio, Ontario
Vocals recorded at Sekret Studios, Missouri
Project custodian: Jim Crichton
Mixed and mastered by Brian Foraker
Front cover artwork created by Alexander Ahilov
Band photo and layout by Alexander Mertsch
Penny Crichton: Pocket Change pictures and artwork coordination
Running time 52:36
Release date: 12 March 2021
Label: earMusic
Highest chart places: DE: 11, CN: did not chart, US: did not chart, UK: did not chart

Powerplay magazine, in February 2021 (237), featured Steve Swift's interview with Michael Sadler. Swift gave the album nine out of ten: 'The brilliant band who delighted us and were due to go, until we wouldn't let them, have produced a sort of new album, *Symmetry*. This is not just an acoustic album; it's a rearranging of those songs we love and opens them up to show how wonderful they are.' Michael Sadler agrees:

> These are not covers. We're not just saying let's take some of our better-known songs and do acoustic versions of them and if those same people give themselves a chance to listen to it, they'll realise it's something special. From a vocal perspective, it was one of the most challenging things I've had to do because when you start playing in a different format, you can't apply the same vocal approach from earlier in your career – you've got to be another guy. That was probably the trickiest part for me.

He continued to explain that choosing the correct instruments was vital so that they worked well together, such as the woodwind and strings, the latter including the banjo, acoustic guitar and mandolin. Jim Gilmour plays piano, accordion and clarinet and there's a fiddle and cellos. Mike Thorne played pretty much whatever was in front of him, including kitchen utensils. He added:

> There are a few hoedown moments and songs where I had to adjust the melody. 'Wind Him Up' is a good example; it was softer with more dynamics. I had to change the melodies to suit.

Jim Crichton was the custodian of the album, collecting all the tracks, which eventually resulted in a standalone record of incredible quality. Being also a fan of folk music and in particular its relationship with prog rock, I was really looking forward to this album. I had wondered why they hadn't done something similar previously, like the old *MTV Unplugged* series at least. The songs are performed with more intimacy, but are still experimental due to the instrumentation and the recording environment.

'Pitchman' (5.18)

'Pitchman' is similar to the original, but done in an infectious 'Hill Billy' style. The song's melody and signature motifs are preserved, thankfully and it does have a new lease of life. Plenty of instruments have been thrust onto the track and it's amazing how they have enriched it purely through this acoustic interpretation. The accordion, fiddle and flute solos are awesome, Crichton's bass is relentlessly soothing and Crichton the younger excels across the many stringed instruments in his repertoire, using a lot of acoustic guitar, mandolin and banjo. Mike Thorne keeps it tight with hot rods/brushes. The pacier instrumental section is a treat and even the mid-section build-up works wonderfully. A brilliantly whimsical opener. Smiles all round.

'The Perfect Time To Feel Better' (8.14)

The first medley on the album turns three songs into a seamless suite. These are more intimate than the originals; the vocal delivery in particular is softer and more introspective than the rock versions.

'Time To Go'

There's quite a lot going on in the first few seconds, with a terrific arrangement of acoustic guitar, piano, clarinet and subtle percussion, but it settles nicely into the track's recognisable melody and the endearing legato piano chords. With the wonderful waltz time signature and the exquisite fiddle refrains, this track benefits from being stripped back. It's a pity they didn't do the whole version.

'The Perfectionist'

It's astonishing how close to the debut album version this is. It's warm and wholesome with a beautiful arrangement and once more, Shane Cook excels on fiddle.

'We Hope You're Feeling Better'

Just 1.06 left for this little ditty, which is cleverly segwayed. It's mainly the chorus repeated, first by Sadler, then chanted by the others.

'Images (Chapter 1)' (4.56)

They just had to include 'Images', not only because it's an excellent track and true reflection of the essence of Saga, but it's the first 'Chapter' and the beginning of the 16-track story. It's also a song that absolutely lends itself to acoustic treatment and it's magnificently presented here, retaining the original structure. As Steve Swift from *Powerplay* magazine (237) observed, 'it's the clarinet that lifts the melody and it's dreamy'. Sadler tones down the vocals, adopting a more talkative, storytelling style, intimate and theatrical. Listen carefully, too, for the kitchen percussion, Thorne being subtle and effective, but it's difficult to identify the specific utensils, possibly spoons! Harmonies add extra texture when the beat picks up and the instrumental section is fabulous. This is more medieval than sci-fi.

'Always There' (4.08)

'Here we go, again', says Sadler as the song begins to pick up momentum. The composition is the same as the original and we're presented here with the full song. Mike Thorne's free-flowing ability manifests with a range of exquisite snare flourishes, propelling the track. Perhaps not an obvious choice to include, as it wasn't a single, a live stalwart, or selected as a 'greatest hit', but it's a very good song. This version was released as a video and can be found on YouTube.

'Prelude #1' (0.49) (Ian Crichton)

Recorded in a cave high in the hills. Probably not, but that's the ambience this short, classical acoustic number invokes. It's Ian Crichton in fine fettle, caressing the strings and creating sumptuous harmonics.

'Say Goodbye To Hollywood' (5.04)

Hypnotic acoustic guitar opens as an alternative to the *Steel Umbrellas* version and it's almost unrecognisable as being the same number. It's replaced momentarily by an accordion serving up the familiar primary melody. Gilmour's vocals are even more tender and vulnerable, befitting this arrangement. There's a gentle rhythm and sweet cymbal splashes courtesy of Thorne and Jim Crichton's bass is uplifting. Perfectly placed is the Hawaiian guitar solo, a prelude to the acoustic guitar and violin motifs.

'Prelude #2' (0.51) (Ian Crichton)

Another compact track, following on from 'Prelude #1', seemingly recorded at the same time in the same environment, with plenty of echo creating the same atmosphere. Crichton reaches further into his acoustic collection, with a fine demonstration of picking intensity whilst creating space between the notes, this particular exemplar being a blend of classical and folk. It reminded me of Jan Ackerman and that is a compliment. They both play tastefully and melodically, focusing on atmosphere, dynamics and creating the right mood for the occasion.

'The Right Side Of The Other Hall' (5.46)

As soon as 'Prelude #2' ends, this track, a montage of three carefully selected songs, comes dashing in. Steve Swift commented that the 'Irish-sounding fiddle and woodwind breakdown is lovely and lifting.'

'Footsteps In The Hall'

I was so pleased to see this number on the list. It's a pity it's not the full version, but this will do and even though it only lasts for just 52 seconds, it features some of the best bits of the song. The melody still radiates and Sadler has a smooth, almost whispered falsetto. The key instrumental segments have been chosen and are still powerful even when played acoustically; the accenting in particular is wonderful.

'You Were Right'

It would appear that this part of the track and the next have been switched on *Symmetry*'s listing. Both are from *Trust* and are in the right order there. This is a superb rendition mirroring the electric format in every aspect. At 2.47, Saga takes us off-track and it's a majestic contrast. The chaps return to their Celtic routes for an all-out Irish folk assault of the highest order. Fiddle, guitars and clarinet are in full flight and as an admirer of this genre, I'm thinking Horslips. This is truly magnificent, but it's all too short.

'On The Other Side'

Another flawless transition into the next sub-track as bass guitar and drums escort the divine folk instrumental into 'On The Other Side' with 2:24 left in this section. It's almost identical to the *Trust* version, as though it's been transported and remixed, with added vocal interplay, Sadler adapting the melody and a piano ending. It's that good, you'll want to go back to the original immediately.

'La Forêt Harmonieuse' (2.00) (Jim Gilmour)

It's a grand piano affair with Gilmour displaying his significant and wide-ranging keyboard techniques, taking us through a classical-infused journey. Thorne interjects with occasional cymbal flourishes and Sadler with random lines from Saga lyrics of the past.

'Wind Him Up' (5:08)

Possibly the only really obvious choice from the list of Saga tracks due to the popularity of the song and the success of its host album. As such, it's a well-considered song for this outing, coming from *Worlds Apart,* which had a more electronic production, mainly from the drums. The acoustic guitar plays the main melody and Sadler is more talkative as the narrator. Sympathetic harmonies, rigorous enthusiastic strumming and the unforgettable chorus are splendid, but with 40 seconds to go, it really takes off. High energy and enjoyment oozes from this short but impactful instrumental segment, with drums, bass and fiddle at the forefront. It was released as a video and it's marvellous.

'No Regrets (Chapter 5)' (3.46)

A near carbon copy of the *Worlds Apart* version, but with different instruments and cutlery that cuts through (pun intended). Gilmour sings and plays the clarinet magnificently. Cellos and violin complement the band admirably, blending with piano, guitar and that awesome clarinet.

'Tired World (Chapter 6)' (6.24)

Sadly, this may be the last ever studio album by Saga and so the closing song should therefore be a cracker and my word it is. They've left the best until last. Saga transport us back to the last track of album number one (43 years ago) and it's a 'Chapter'. That's a smart move. It's a brilliant song anyway, but this reimagining is stupendous. It's in parallel with the *Saga* recording, but somehow has added intensity and dynamics and it couldn't be any tighter. Sadler is in full voice and the acoustic guitar pans across the speakers to add more energy. A banjo has never sounded sweeter, but it's in the hands of Ian Crichton and what a solo, well worth the album's price alone. Quite rightly, this was released as a terrific video.

Live Albums And DVDs

I've included as accurately as I can all the Saga live releases in date order. The lineup is Michael Sadler, Jim Crichton, Ian Crichton, Steve Negus and Jim Gilmour, unless otherwise stated.

In Transit (1982) (Polydor)

From the *Worlds Apart* tour, recorded at Rudi-Sedlmayer Hall in Munich on 5 February 1982 and Tivoli Concert Hall in Copenhagen on 22, 23 and 24 February 1982. Produced by Jim Crichton.

Following the success of *Worlds Apart* and with the band's popularity growing on both sides of the Atlantic, Saga recorded their first live album with sound engineer Dieter Derks on a 32-track mobile digital recording studio. *In Transit* became the first fully digital live rock album ever to be released on CD. Jim Crichton experienced a steep learning curve, not only in producing a live album but also in trying to understand the digital nuances. The album was expensive to make but was well worth it, showcasing the band's songwriting and performing prowess and accurately capturing their interactions with an appreciative audience. All future Saga live albums would be recorded directly from the soundboard and mixed on Crichton's laptop. *In Transit* achieved Gold status in Canada on 23 October and Platinum in January 1983.

The production is superb and the performances are immaculate, almost identical to the studio versions. There are nine tracks, including the newbie 'A Brief Case'. The standout song is 'Humble Stance'; also memorable is Gilmour's clarinet on 'No Regrets'. Live albums were all the rage at the time and this is as good as any. It was reissued by earMusic in 2021.

'A Brief Case' (2.19) (Sadler, Negus)

A drum duet featuring Negus on his Simmons and Sadler on an electronically modified flight case (Roland Octopad II). It's a great live spectacle and the audio is captured well here, particularly the panning from speaker to speaker. Negus is an exceptional drummer, laying down the main beat for Sadler. They also solo well together and the enthusiastic crowd enjoy chanting along. A worthy inclusion.

Detours (1998) (SPV/Steamhammer)

Produced by Jim Crichton, the album was recorded on the 1997 *Pleasure And The Pain* tour. It features eight shows in Germany, Austria and France. The gig in Offenbach, on 13 June 1997, officially marked Saga's 20th live anniversary and the 15th anniversary of *In Transit*. *Detours* contains 22 songs, with two new tracks, a rendition of 'In The Hall Of The Mountain King William' and 'William's Walk About', the latter showcasing Gilmour's brilliance on the piano. Sadler is terrific as the frontman and the production is tight. The best tracks are 'The Interview' and 'The Perfectionist'. It was reissued by earMusic in 2021, the vinyl version being an impressive triple package.

'In The Hall Of The Mountain King William' (2.46) (Edvard Grieg)
The opening track to whip up the crowd and give the band time to get organised before they launch into 'How Long'. It's an instrumental for the 'Peer Gynt Suite' by Norwegian Grieg. Saga's version starts with a loud click track and Ian Critchton seemingly warming up with a shredding exercise. At 0.44, the band join in with a crescendo, solid accenting and a few random shouts from Sadler before the song begins in earnest and it's heavy, the main feature being Crichton's guitar riffs and soloing. It's not bad and gets the band and their crew ready for the rest of the concert.

'William's Walk About' (2.39) (J. Gilmour)
Track 11 is an instrumental performed by Gilmour alone on the keyboards with a piano effect. He starts with an extract from 'Images (Chapter 1)' from *Images At Twilight* before moving through a range of classical-based pieces and the ending of 'No Stranger (Chapter 8)' from *Worlds Apart*. It's an exceptional display of musicianship and showmanship.

Silhouette (2003) (SPV/Steamhammer)
A DVD containing ten videos available for the first time to the public, including an unreleased video of 'Always There' made exclusively for the 25th anniversary of Saga. There are also ten live tracks, three being 'bootlegs' filmed in the UK and a 2002 interview with the band. It's the first time Saga had released any live footage.

The interviews were filmed over a period of five months in four different countries and chronicle the history of the band from 1977 to 2002. It was the first time Saga fans could own footage of the band playing live and actually see and hear them talking about how it all began, with the bonus of access to unseen videos. It's a fabulous DVD on many levels, further connecting Saga with their fans.

Marathon World Tour 2003 – The Official Bootleg (2003) (Eclipse Media Group)
A DVD with a 12-song concert and bonus features: a tour photo gallery, an acoustic 'Rise And Shine' live at the Berns and a TV performance of 'On The Loose'. The DVD project came together during a break in touring on the *Marathon* world tour. The band reviewed hours of video and thousands of photos from the tour, none of it shot with the intention of a DVD. There are no corrections or overdubs on this show and at times, the band didn't even know they were being filmed. The picture quality is a bit grainy and slightly off colour, but the sound is very good.

There are plenty of multi-angle shots, but the editing lacks continuity and the audience, at times, seem quietly stunned by the performances, which are marvellous. The video ends with footage of Saga setting up for rehearsal with Christian Simpson.

Live In Bonn 2002 – All Areas (2004) (SPV/Steamhammer)
A limited-edition double DVD celebrating Saga's 25th anniversary with a one-off open-air show in Bonn. It contains 16 tracks with bonus features: a discography, a photo gallery, a making-of documentary and a description of the gear used. It also includes the *Marathon World Tour 2003 DVD* (see above). It comes with a four-page leaflet, with credits typed in red over a series of photographs, making it almost impossible to read. The editing is abysmal. A black screen appears after every song, clearly suggesting that the songs are not presented in the order they were performed. It's a shame because everything else is just right. The visuals and camera angles are brilliant, especially the close-up and birds-eye view of the multitude of Korg keyboards, but they do get too close to Ian Crichton occasionally. The audience is enthusiastic and the playing and setlist are superb.

The Chapters Live (2005) (SPV)
A double CD featuring all 16 'Chapter' songs played in numerical order. The 36-page booklet is so thick that it's hard to get in and out of the crystal case without damaging it. It's stunning though and oozes quality, with each track having its own exquisite illustration by Eric Fulghum aside each lyric, with further conceptual insights from Jim Crichton. The booklet, with its terrific cover by Penny Crichton, is worth twice the price of the CD on its own and it would have made a fantastic vinyl package. Gilmour's clarinet on 'No Regrets' is outstanding and the twin lead on 'Uncle Albert's Eyes' is astonishing. Standout tracks are 'Will It Be You', 'Tired World' and 'Too Much To Lose'. There isn't much commentary between songs, so the opportunity to narrate and further explain the 'Chapters' has been missed.

Worlds Apart Revisited (2007) (SPV/Inside Out)
The two DVD package contains a full concert recorded on 8 December 2005 in Pratteln, Switzerland. There are 22 live songs, all nine from *Worlds Apart*, played in order, sandwiched in the middle of an excellent set from other albums. The second DVD has *Worlds Apart Road Stories*, five live performances from England in 1981, *Worlds Apart Revisited Documentary* and a photo gallery. The 16-page booklet has lyrics from the entire set and a range of photos. This release (apart from *Live In England*) features Brian Doerner on drums. 'Live In England' doesn't have the same quality, but is just as enjoyable, the performances being sublime. This was also available as a CD package without the bonuses.

Contact Live In Munich (2009) (DVD/CD/Both) (SPV/Inside Out)
Michael Sadler's final concert in Germany, filmed at Muffathalle in Munich. The DVD package has four discs – two audio, two visual – covering exactly the same 21 songs and superb drum and piano solos. DVD Disc 2 – Saga B-Roll – is a bonus covering a further live concert with six songs recorded for

underground TV, live in Mannheim; a video of Jim Gilmour talking about the Saga landmarks in Toronto and Ian Crichton talking about their relationship with Munich; and a photo gallery of the 30th anniversary tour and the farewell show of Michael Sadler.

It has an eight-page booklet with some great individual live photos. The two middle pages have been dedicated to the drummer for the tour, Chris Sutherland and his impressive Sonor double bass drum kit. A nice gesture from the band. The CD is the same, but with no bonuses, so you're better off with the DVD, which is beautifully packaged and befitting Michael Sadler's farewell. It's a magnificent set chosen from most of the albums to date. Sadler opens up appropriately with 'Always There', but his vocals could have been louder. Chris Sutherand's style leans more towards straight rock, but he's got all the chops. Sadler is emotional as the audience sings 'Bye-bye Michael' and the band and crew present him with flowers. 'I don't know what to say, thank you' and 'Until we meet again'.

Heads Or Tails Live (2011) (earMusic)
This is the whole *Heads Or Tails* album recorded live and presented in the same order as the studio version, with no additional songs and no bonuses. It features Rob Moratti on vocals, the first and only live release without Michael Sadler. Moratti is therefore singing songs he didn't write or record. Brian Doerner is on drums, a class act with super fills and powerful double-kick drumming. The CD is a digipak with details spread over three sides of the foldable cover. The text is small, but clear, with live photos on the front and back cover. It's a great album full of exceptional performances and you can really hear the differences in vocal styles and delivery, especially on 'Social Orphan'. The finest track is 'The Intermission', which suits Moratti's voice the most. He and Gilmour harmonise well, especially on 'Scratching The Surface'.

Spin It Again Live In Munich (2013) (CD and DVD) (earMusic)
Filmed in Muffathalle in November 2012. Michael Sadler is back and having released *20/20* in 2012, Saga are on the road in the same year. Sadler announces 'Five years ago, I said goodbye. Five years later, I'm here to say hello.' The album houses 19 songs, including 'Fish Beat', a drum solo by Mike Thorne on his first official recorded output with Saga – a splendid demonstration of linear and rudimental drumming. It's not an obvious set, with some new material to complement some old stagers. The DVD package comes with a bonus 'Behind the Scenes'. The eight-page booklet has concert photos, track listings, credits and details of the crew. The CD is a replica and comes as a two-CD pack.

Live At SWR1 Rockarena 2013 (2014) (earMusic)
A bonus concert within the limited-edition digipack CD of *Sagacity*. Titled *CD2 Saga Hits,* you can probably guess which nine tracks were selected. Only

'Mouse In A Maze' and 'The Cross' seem like atypical choices to me, the latter being the absolute standout track.

Live In Hamburg (2016) (earMusic)
Recorded at the Fabrik, Hamburg, on 28 April 2015. The two-CD digipack has no booklet, just a track listing and basic credits and disappointingly, there are no photos from the show. The vinyl edition is a much better proposition. Two LPs housed in gatefold sleeves with 30 individually posed portrait photos and live images on the inner cover. It's a greatest hits set of 16 songs, but it only has 'I'll Be' from *Sagacity*. Highlights include the instrumental section on 'Hot To Cold', Gilmour's solo piano montage, 'Scratching The Surface' and the inclusion of 'Someone Should'.

Live At The Montreal Forum (2018) (Air Cuts)
An obscure release not part of the mainstream portfolio by the band or their several previous labels. The CD looks professional enough, with an interesting cover of a giant alien beetle destroying a city, so it's got the *Images At Twilight* appeal. There's an eight-page booklet with a small range of band photos through the ages and some notes giving a very brief precis of Saga and the track selection. The 80 minutes of music (16 tracks) on this disc features songs from their albums of the late 1970s and early 1980s. The show took place during their *Heads Or Tails* tour in 1983, their only album to make the Canadian top 20. 'This broadcast captures Saga's best lineup at their peak'. The poor soundboard quality masks a superb set, so it's still worth owning.

So Good So Far – Live At Rock Of Ages (2018) (CD/DVD and Vinyl) (earMusic)
A concert celebrating 40 years of Saga, consisting of 16 tracks in a two-CD and DVD bonus package, recorded at the Rock of Ages Festival on 29 July 2017. The 16-page booklet is mainly made up of concert footage and pictures. The vinyl is double gatefold and part of earMusic's 2021 reissues; it doesn't have any bonuses, but it does have liner notes by Michael Sadler, so I'd get both CD/DVD and vinyl packages. Sadler in the album sleeve notes:

> Saga has a very special history with the legendary Rock of Ages festival in Seebronn, Germany. We performed for the very first time in 2006. Fast forward to 2007, Saga returns to the coveted Saturday night stage by special request, celebrating the band's 40th anniversary with our final *Chapter* tour. This release captures the sound and atmosphere of that spectacular night with our musical family and friends that will never be repeated … or will it?

The sound and visuals are up to the usual standard, as are the performances, production editing and camera angles. Mike Thorne is behind the kit, full of energy and his colleagues are also animated, with Sadler being expressive.

Also on the bill that day were Marillion and Pretty Maids. In 2006, it included Twisted Sister, Wishbone Ash, Uriah Heap and UFO.

Compilations

In common with all Saga albums and singles, there have been several reissues across different labels, territories and formats. It would be fruitless to list all the tracks and credits for each song within these compilations, as they are expertly catalogued on several Saga-related websites and other resources, some highlighted in the bibliography.

Saga (Amiga) (1985)
Ten tracks from the first four albums with a total running time of 41.02. Not to be confused with Saga's first self-titled album, this is a compilation made in Germany for the German Market with liner notes by Barbara Lammel. It features a great cover photo from the *Heads Or Tails* tour – it's worth owning the vinyl version just for that. I managed to get mine from an antique shop for £5.

Times Up (Polydor) (1986)
This features 11 tracks from the first five albums, totalling 48 minutes, with an LP cover by Gerd Huss that displays a strange computer, sci-fi, space theme on both sides, one side being more organic with a plant 'caressing' the machine. This bears no relation to anything Saga had done. A great choice of songs, though.

The Works (BMG/Bonaire) (1991)
A stonking 28 tracks make this great value for money, but disappointingly, there is no booklet on the band or any photos. However, there is a good mix of tracks from most of the albums released at the time, including live tracks from *In Transit* and the singles 'Gotta Love It', 'The Call' and 'Solsbury Hill'.

Wind Him Up (Zounds) (1992)
Another German compilation, with 16 tracks amassing just over 74 minutes of some obvious and some not-so-obvious songs. It's a great booklet, with a black and white picture of a very young-looking Saga and three photos from later in their career. Liner notes are by Volker Koerdt. It also advertises other albums from the series, including Kansas, Journey and REO Speedwagon.

All The Best 1978 To 1993 (Quality Music) (1993)
Compiled by Markus Klinke, the painting is by Ioannis and the photos were taken by Penny Crichton. The album houses 15 tracks at 69 minutes and was distributed in Canada.

The cover artwork shows the front covers of *Saga, Images At Twilight, Heads Or Tails* and *The Security Of Illusion* and the song selection is cracking, with *Worlds Apart* contributing the most songs, so it's strange that this cover isn't shown.

Defining Moments Volume 1 (Bonaire) (1994)
A four-page booklet has all the information you need to know about the 15 tracks chosen. There are some errors. 'Odd Man Out' is not from *Worlds Apart*. There's info on the Saga fan club. We're still awaiting volume two!

The Very Best Of (Polydor) (1994)
A folding orange, yellow and pink poster replaces the usual booklet to provide the necessary information. Despite lacking any band photos, there are some interesting pictures by 'Vivid Images' using bubbles to capture three album covers, including *Steel Umbrellas*. The 15 tracks are a fine selection, but not really the very best.

Wildest Dreams (Spectrum) (1995)
Clearly done on a small budget and distributed in Germany, this includes a four-page booklet, with a small picture of the band on the cover and a list of the 14 tracks inside, with one quarter of the middle pages being an advert for a Philips CD Sound Machine. Page four lists other Stars of the World, including Black Sabbath, Connie Francis, Richard Clayderman and Uriah Heep.

How Do I Look? (Spectrum) (1996)
Spectrum are at it again. Only one year after *Wildest Dreams* comes *How Do I Look?*. Here we have another 14 tracks, including duplicates from its predecessor, but that's not sufficient to put you off adding this to your collection. The booklet is similar, with the Stars of the World lineup, but the front cover is much better with a vintage live photograph.

Remember When – The Very Best Of Saga (Steamhammer/SPV) (2006)
Astonishingly, it's been ten years since the last compilation album. This 'Best Of' is professionally presented by SPV, with 26 tracks selected from a deeper pool of Saga's portfolio. The front cover is mainly the Saga logo and the CDs themselves are imprinted with the *Chapters Live* image, which is also on the back cover. The six-page booklet has excellent, detailed liner notes detailing the band's history. There is no information regarding who compiled or designed the package, but the selection is excellent, nonetheless.

The Collection (Universal/Polydor) (2013)
Saga at this stage in their career have over 200 original compositions to choose from and it's been seven years since the last compendium. Thirty-six tracks sit across a triple CD, so a marathon to complete it in one sitting. Musically, there are no problems at all, but the minimalist booklet is really poor. There's sufficient detail about each track, but nothing about Saga.

Now And Then The Collection – 1978 To Infinity (earMusic) (2015)
A high-quality, cleverly compiled double CD featuring 21 tracks, one chosen from every studio album so far. It's a fantastic concept, even though I'd disagree with most of those chosen, but that's the appeal; it makes you think about your own favourite track from each Saga album and therefore is an absolute must buy. The booklet is a glorious 20 pages, including all the lyrics, album covers, song credits, lots of photos through the ages, posters, concert tickets and miniature extracts of articles. All songs were remastered in 2015, so worth it for that alone.

The Polydor Legacy (Universal/Polydor) (2017)
Polydor cash in with a single CD of 17 tracks. It's got an appealing light blue cover and poster-style booklet with an old Saga logo in bold red adorning the front. A good variety of tracks is taken from the first eight studio albums in chronological order. There are no band credits, but there are four small photos on the back of the booklet. It'll do.

The Best Of – All The Hits Since 1978 (earMusic) (2021)
The last one for now, but I imagine there'll be at least one more before Saga decide to hang up their keyboards. It's been four years since the last compilation CD and this should have been the best of the best, but it's not. It's got 25 of the hits and they are immaculate choices, including two bonus tracks from *Symmetry*, which is a nice little taster, but where's the booklet or the information to support its release? Just enjoy the music.

Box Sets/Bundles
Two Originals Of Saga – *Full Circle, House Of Cards* (Steamhammer) (2005)
Two Originals Of Saga – *Marathon, Network* (Steamhammer) (2008)
Two Originals Of Saga – *In Transit, Silent Knight* (Polydor) (2010)
Five Original Albums – *Wildest Dreams, How Do I Look, Heads Or Tails, Images At Twilight, Behaviour* (Polydor) (2013)
Five Original Albums – *Saga, Silent Knight, Worlds Apart, In Transit, Pleasure And The Pain* (Polydor) (2015)
Collectors Package – *20/20, Spin It Again – Live In Munich, Sagacity* (earMusic) (2015)

Solo Albums

There are no surprises in individual style, genre, musicianship, writing ability and sheer excellence. I've added credits if another member of the Saga family is involved. You might discover different versions.

Michael Sadler

1998 – *Back Where You Belong* (Self-Release) – Limited edition signed and numbered.
2004 – *Clear* (MSI Records) – Also released in the same year as a limited edition, signed and numbered. Recorded at Sound Image Studios. Additional vocals by Gwen Sadler, who is also an executive producer. Additional engineering by Jim Crichton.
2014 – *One Clear Night* (MSI Records) – Ian Crichton on guitar.

Ian Crichton

1995 – *Welcome To The Boom Boom Room* (No Bull Records) – Production assisted by Steve Negus, who also plays guitar on one track. Cover photo by Penny Crichton.
1997 – *Ghettos By Design* (USG Records)
2022 – *Six By Six* – Six By Six (Inside Out)
2024 – *Six By Six* – Beyond Shadowland (Inside Out)

Steve Negus And Jim Gilmour

1989 – *Gilmore Negus Project (GNP)* – Safety Zone – Reissued in 2006 and 2022. Recorded and mixed at Phase One Studio, produced by Steve Negus.

Steve Negus

2008 – *Dare To Dream* (Cyclone Records – Self Release) – Jim Gilmour on keyboards.
2023 – *Economy Of Motion* (Self Release) – Peter Rochon plays piano on one track and Nicole Negus sings on one track and is in the 'Negus Choir'.

Jim Gilmour

1996 – James Gerrard Gilmour – *Instrumental Encounters* (Eclipse)
2005 – *The Great Escape* (Progrock Records) – Reissued in 2006 as a second edition with a different cover. Christian Simpson plays drums on three tracks. Album cover concept and design by Penny Crichton.

Time To Go

Saga took a well-earned rest following their monumental *It Never Ends* tour and their performances on Cruise to the Edge on 4 April 2025. This was a different-looking Saga than the one that set off on the journey in 1977. Still a band of awesome musicians, joining Sadler, Gilmour and Thorne were Dusty Chesterfield (guitar) and Mike Borkosky (bass). Their last tour performance was in Pratteln, Switzerland, on 7 December 2024. An immaculate set, they opened with an intro medley and closed the final encore with 'You're Not Alone'.

The band recently announced two concerts in Canada in the summer of 2026, followed by a series of European dates to celebrate their 50th anniversary, *1977-2027: The Generations* tour. Hopefully, they'll do more to mark this extraordinary milestone. Just a few suggestions, if I may, not in any particular order: play in the UK, create a stage production or film of *Generation 13* and/or the 'Chapters' saga, release a box set of unreleased material and have an almighty reunion. Good luck.

Interviews

Interview with Steve Negus (23 August 2024)

Q: In terms of your drumming style, how would somebody know it was you playing?

A: I think I have a recognisable style that probably comes from my R&B background, which made Saga different from all the other progressives. I'm playing R&B grooves underneath a progressive rock band. It just gave Saga a completely different shape than, say, Yes or King Crimson.

Q: Who would you say Saga were like, who you were compared to?

A: We were listening to Supertramp, Gentle Giant, Emerson, Lake & Palmer when I was younger. I don't know whether we actually sounded like them. Definitely Supertramp with the keyboards, which was very interesting. I saw them in Quebec City and it was awesome. Chris de Burgh was the opener. I ended up, years later, working with Chris on *The Getaway* album.

Q: Great drummer, Supertramp's.

A: Not many people know his name (Bob Siebenberg), but I love his playing on *Crime Of The Century*. He's such a player and an influence on me, too. He played all the right stuff; his grooves were wonderful.

Q: What is your fondest memory with Saga?

A: I think doing Rock Am Ring in Nuremberg with 200,000 people there – the biggest festival in Germany. We did that a couple of times.

Q: For someone who's never heard of Saga before, what album would you recommend that represents the band?

A: Probably the first one. That's when we were shaping the whole sound of Saga. Peter Rochon's contributions should not be overlooked. He actually did play a couple of tracks on my latest album, *Economy Of Motion*.

Q: What's your favourite Saga track?

A: That's a tough one – there are so many! I would say tracks that stand out are 'Humble Stance'. It's that R&B thing, a cut time shuffle. It's really a typical funk move. I don't think we ever played a show without playing 'Humble Stance' and 'Take A Chance' was a good one off of *Behaviour*.

Q: That's interesting, choosing one from *Behaviour*.

A: The thing I like most about 'Take A Chance' is that it probably best captured my drum sound. Peter Walsh produced and we decided to go to Munich to Union Studios, which is an old studio with a great sounding room, really high ceilings. 'Take A Chance' is really the essence of what I do in a nutshell.

Q: I have some very fond memories of my first Saga gig at Hammersmith Odeon. Any thoughts from that concert?

A: When we played the Hammersmith Odeon, Lemmy used to hang out at the backstage bar, which was his local. Somebody asked him to do a review of the Saga show and he said, 'The lights flashed green and red.' That was it. Speaking of Motorhead, Mickey D was a big Saga fan and still is. He used to play all the Saga CDs on the tour bus, so Lemmy was sick of hearing us.

Q: Your only concept album was *Generation 13*. Have you got a quick overview for us?

A: It's just really about how our generation screwed it all up. There's a father, a son and a puppet. The puppet has a personality and the father is abusive to his son, so his son kind of reflects more towards the puppet. It's a very dark album, but it's really just talking about the different generations. There are some great tracks on there. 'The Learning Tree' is very cool. I enjoyed making that album.

Q: I jotted down all the songs you've been involved with in terms of the writing process. How would you describe your input?

A: I was writing a lot of music and playing keyboards. Daryl and I were working on stuff together. We would bring in our 'bits' and collectively pick out certain ones that everybody liked to work on. So 'Learning Tree' is pretty much what I brought to the band. 'No Strings Attached' was another one that Daryl and I had worked on. I've always contributed to the writing in the initial stages, usually in the rehearsal room. When we were Pockets, we spent eight months together, writing what became the first album and part of the second album. We just hashed things out.

Q: How did you get into engineering, producing and mastering (the 2002 reissues)?

A: I used to program a lot of Daryl sounds. It's all just a logical extension of what I do, whether it's keyboards or any instrument; music is music and I'll wear all the different hats. I got into engineering initially because a lot of engineers couldn't capture my drum sound. I found the best way to do anything is to do it yourself. We had to remaster the entire catalogue, so I just did it at home. I sent Jimmy Crichton copies to sign off on them.

Q: There was that transition in Saga's music during the decades and you seem to change with the mood of each era.

A: You have to do that; it's all part of keeping the interest. We would upset the fans sometimes; one album is too commercial and then the next one's too progressive. That's all part and parcel of the process.

Q: That's been fantastic, Steve, thanks so much.

A: If you have any more questions, just give me a holler.

Steve then mentioned that straight after our discussion, he was off to see Saga in concert at the Aurora RibFest in Hamilton, the first time he'd seen them for some time. I asked him to give them my best.

Interview with Jim Crichton (28 October 2024)

Q: It's brilliant to talk to you and you'll have seen how the *On Track* series works. There's even one for *Gentle Giant*. I'll buy it for you.

A: I didn't see that one, but that's pretty cool.

Q: Your introduction to the bass guitar is well documented, but how did you get into keyboards?

A: I was playing in a band on the East Coast of Canada and a Stevie Wonder song came on – I can't remember which – and I heard this amazing bass sound. I thought, 'That's the coolest bass I've heard in a long time.' I thought, 'I need to do that.' It was a Moog. I'd never heard it before, but I managed to track one down, found out where the C note was and all the other notes, so I started to play Moog bass in that band. That was before Saga, but I still like having it as another sound; it's a great instrument to play.

Q: You swapped with Ian, who was playing bass initially.

A: I had an old Guild guitar and Ian kept coming into my room and pinching my bass and did quite well with it, but I said, 'No, no, we're not having two bass players. This is your guitar' and I gave him the six-string and shut the door. And it worked out really well.

Q: When playing live, you swap between bass and Moog. How do you decide which to play for each song?

A: I grew up as a bass guitar player; the Moog is just for texture. There are certain things that a Moog can do that a guitar can't. I could shake the side of a building with a Moog. I can go into the dressing room after the show and find ceiling tiles all over (laughs). The low-end frequency is extremely low. So it depends on what type of song it is, how it hits me and I'll try both until one works.

Q: Would you say you've got a signature style in terms of playing bass?

A: No, not really. I like to stay on the melodic side of things. When we started Saga, I had a meeting with Steve and I said, 'Look, the guitar player and the keyboard player are going completely whacky all the time, so I thought it would be a good idea for the drums and bass to keep it fairly simple.' So when we're looking at a room full of people and they're jumping up and down to the simple drums and bass, it works. If the drums and bass acted like the guitar and keyboards in Saga, we would have been a fusion band and sold about three records.

Q: What would you say is your favourite bass part in a Saga song?

A: Oh, there's a whole bunch of them. The other day, I was playing the middle section of a song called 'Runaway', which is a really good finger exercise for anyone who wants to play bass. It's got a running bass pattern in the middle of the song. It's a great exercise.

Q: Do you have a favourite Saga song? I know that's an obvious question.

A: No, there are way too many.

Q: Any particular track that you liked to play live?

A: Well, some of them we'd play thousands of times, so they just come naturally, muscle memory, so I don't have to think about it. I suppose it depends on what year it is and what we've done to the arrangement. We'll do some arranging and add some different bits, but there are so many songs that I like playing. That's the good part about writing the tunes, I just like playing them.

Q: Is there a record that you're most proud of?

A: Well, I really like what happened with *Generation 13,* which was pretty wild and unnecessarily crazy. At the time, I thought, 'There is no chance in hell that we'll get on the radio, so let's just do what we want', so we made that album, which was a lot of fun

Q: Had you thought the album could become a show?

A: I've actually designed stages for that exact purpose, but I don't know if it will ever happen. I did start working on ideas for it.

Q: What would be something to behold for the fans?

A: Well, I have a couple of ideas for a different setup. One of them is incorporating an orchestra pit in front of the band, but instead of an orchestra being there, I'd have five to ten keyboards. One would be cellos, one would be piccolos, one would be violas and just have ten guys down there that are the orchestra. Now that you can get keyboards to imitate an orchestra, it would be fairly hard to tell the difference. That was one of the ideas to perform these things live.

Q: Am I okay to put that in the book?

A: Oh, sure and somebody else might do it.

Q: When you're writing your own songs, what tends to come first: the music or the lyrics?

A: Almost always the music. It's better to get the music to help you to figure out what you're saying. I remember seeing something on the Bee Gees and they worked to get the melody in stone before someone produced the lyrics. If there was one extra syllable that didn't fit, they'd throw the lyrics in the garbage. They would not change the melody and I guess it all worked out well for them. I thought that was pretty cool

Q: Speaking of the Bee Gees, didn't they release an album on the same label about the same time as Saga's first album?

A: When we put out the first album, it was doing okay in Germany and around and they were cutting the laser in the States. The main guy from Polydor Records told us at the time that this was a great week to release the album, as there was only one other album coming out. So it would be phenomenal for a new band to have all that and it turns out that it was *Saturday Night Fever*. It came out and we just disappeared into the dust (laughs).

Q: Well, they did okay and so did you with the success, particularly in Germany.

A: It was a slow climb, but really neat, and, of course, some of those early songs the band still plays to this day.

Q: Did you know there's only one track from *Saga* and one track from *Images* that don't appear on any of the live albums or DVDs? They're 'Climbing The Ladder' and 'Slow Motion'.

A: Ah, well, 'Slow Motion' is such a pain in the butt for keyboard players; they talk us out of it. It's not hard, it's just monotonous. I'm sure we played it sometime and it appeared quite a lot on the radio over here in Canada.

Q: Is there anything about the 'Chapters' that we might have missed?

A: I've been working on that recently for a couple of things I'm thinking about and hopefully you'll find out later. It's about the things people are aware of, not treating the planet properly. In 1979, I was already alarmed about what we were doing and that's what it's about: an alien race trying to stop us from completely destroying this place. It was an odd thing for a band to do on their first album, but it got people talking, which was good. I didn't know what 'Chapter 8' was, but I guessed we'd figure it out.

Q: And, of course, the whole concept came back, including the aliens, with *Full Circle*.

A: Yes, absolutely and I consider what's in the 'Chapters' to be clues to the stories. I purposely wrote it in a way that people could interpret it. The meat and potatoes of the story were never really stated in any of the songs, but it's hinted at in a large way in some of them. We did get people writing about what they thought the story was about and I would read them in the offices in Toronto and it was amazing what some people came up with, nothing to do with what the 'Chapters' were about. Even if you read all those lyrics, you still won't know what happened. You think you might know, but you're not sure.

Q: For someone who's never heard of Saga before, what album would you recommend that represents Saga?

A: Oh, that's difficult to choose. The obvious one would be *Worlds Apart*. Some great tracks on that and it's a great sound and it was magical to be involved in.

Q: Do you think you could have played in the UK more?

A: The band wanted to, but there were certain areas that just started fading away. I used to live in England for two years and I enjoyed watching how fast England, as a country, can get through a band. You're on *Top Of The Pops* and you're number one. A year later, no one wants to hear you ever again. It's just incredible how quickly a country can devour a band (laughs).

Q: What do you think Saga's legacy will be?

A: I haven't given that any thought. I suppose a band that came up with more albums than most, hung in there and generally made good quality albums from beginning to end. To have a band that made so many studio albums stay intact for over 40 years is something to be proud of. I remember us spending at least a full year on every one of them; we didn't do them quickly

Q: As a producer, do you have a favourite album from that perspective?

A: I just love what we did with Rupert. I learned so much from him. We'd come over from Canada with some respectable albums, used the best gear and we turned up in England to a 200-year-old barn. I questioned everything that was going on when we arrived there and I even said to Rupert, 'When are you guys going to finish the studio?' He looked at me with this horrified face and said, 'We are not touching anything, that's why we built the control room in a place that sounds unbelievable.' And he said, 'There have been a couple of bands in here before you, you know?' He listed a few and it was ridiculous, but the whole experience was kinda cool.

We chatted for a little while longer and talked about Jim's time working with Jon Anderson and what a great experience that was.

Bibliography

Books And Journal Articles

Ammerlaan, E., *Saga: The Biography* (EA Media, 2008)
Edwardson, R., *Canuck Rock: A History Of Canadian Popular Music* (University of Toronto Press, 2009)
Hulmes, P.J., *In Search Of Kim Michell* (Peter Joe Hulmes, 2023)
Melhuish, M., *Heart Of Gold: 30 Years Of Canadian Pop Music* (CNC Enterprises Toronto, 1983)
Melhuish, M., *Oh What A Feeling: A Vital History Of Canadian Music* (Quarry Press, 1996)
Popoff, M., 'Popoff Archive 2: Progressive Rock' (2016)

Magazines

Kerrang!, 1983 (various)
Power Play, 2021
Prog, 2014, 2018, 2021, 2022
Saga, *Heads Or Tails* World Tour Brochure 83/84

Online Resources

sagagen.com
pennycrichtonart.com
michaelsadler.com
stevenegus.com
jimgilmour.net
robmoratti.net
curtcress.com
sixbysixband.com
edwinammerlaan.com
berttreep.com
iopages.nl
martinpopoff.com
bobwegner.ca
facebook.com/SAGAgeneration
saga.works
saga-germany.de
forum.saga-germany.de
rockmusictimeline.com
tonyrobertsart.co.uk
Noisecreep.com

Would you like to write for Sonicbond Publishing?

We are mainly a music publisher, but we also occasionally publish in other genres including film and television. At Sonicbond Publishing we are always on the look-out for authors, particularly for our two main series, On Track and Decades.

Mixing fact with in depth analysis, the On Track series examines the entire recorded work of a particular musical artist or group. All genres are considered from easy listening and jazz to 60s soul to 90s pop, via rock and metal.

The Decades series singles out a particular decade in an artist or group's history and focuses on that decade in more detail than may be allowed in the On Track series.

While professional writing experience would, of course, be an advantage, the most important qualification is to have real enthusiasm and knowledge of your subject. First-time authors are welcomed, but the ability to write well in English is essential.

Sonicbond Publishing has distribution throughout Europe and North America, and all our books are also published in E-book form. Authors will be paid a royalty based on sales of their book. Further details about our books are available from www.sonicbondpublishing.com. To contact us, complete the contact form there or email info@sonicbondpublishing.co.uk